The National Council for
Crime Prevention
Sweden

# The Swedish Code of Judicial Procedure

The translation is that of the wording
of the Code of Judicial Procedure
as at January 1, 1985



Stockholm, May 1985

Report No 16

The National Swedish Council for Crime Prevention (Brottsförebyggande rådet) established 1974, is a government agency under the Ministry of Justice. The Council is headed by a board of 20 persons appointed by the government and representing a wide range of important functions in the community. The Council has an office with a permanent staff.

The address is:
Brottsförebyggande rådet
Atlasmuren 1
S-113 21 STOCKHOLM, Sweden
Telephone: (Stockholm) 08-22 97 80

The Council publishes reports in Swedish and English. The Council also issues abstracts on crime and correction in Sweden.
This report can be ordered from
Liber Förlag
Kundtjänst
S-162 89 STOCKHOLM, Sweden

ISBN 91-38-08845-2
Omslag Förlagsateljén
Produktion AB Allmänna Förlaget
**minab/gotab** Stockholm 1985 81456

# Contents

# Introduction

The Swedish Code of Judicial Procedure came into force in 1948. The code was mainly the result of a reformwork conserning court proceedings. Since that the Swedish Code of Judicial Procedure has been continuously renewed and new revisions are planned. The work has been directed mostly towards organizational questions.

The American Series of Foreign Penal Codes published in 1968 "The Swedish Code of Judicial Procedure" in English translation. The text was translated by Anders Bruzelius, City Court Judge, Lund, Sweden and Ruth Bader Ginsburg, Associate Professor of Law, Rutgers, USA.

In order to have a more up-to-date translation the National Swedish Council for Crime Prevention (NCCP) has brought out a new English edition of the Swedish Code of Judicial Procedure.

In this translation NCCP has proceeded from the 1968 edition of "The Swedish Code of Judicial Procedure" and introduced the amendments and additions that have come into effect since 1967. The entire material has thereafter been reviewed and certain adjustments have been made in order to ensure a uniform terminology.

This translation is the work of John Hogg, authorized translator, and the text is the wording of the Code of Judicial Procedure as at January 1, 1985.

Stockholm, May 1985

*Bo Svensson*
Director of the National Swedish Council
for Crime Prevention

# Part One

# Organization of Courts

## Chapter 1

### General Lower Courts

#### Section 1

The district courts are the general lower courts and, unless otherwise prescribed, the courts of first instance.

The judicial district is the circuit of the district court. The division of the country into judicial districts is prescribed by the Government. (SFS 1974:573)

#### Section 2

In a district court there shall be a district judge and, unless otherwise determined by the Government, one or more assistant district judges. In those district courts which the Government decides there shall also be one or more chief assistant district judges. District judges, chief assistant district judges and assistant district judges shall be learned in law.

A district court may work in divisions. The chairman of a division is the district judge or a chief assistant district judge.

Each district court shall have a clerical office open to the public at fixed times. (SFS 1979:166)

#### Section 3

In the district courts three judges learned in law constitute the bench in civil cases. More than four judges learned in law may not sit in the court.

In criminal cases a district court shall consist of a judge learned in law and a panel of three lay judges. In actions for prosecution of crimes for which the statutory sanction is not more lenient than imprisonment for two years, however, the court shall consist of a judge learned in law and a panel of five lay judges. If necessary by reason of the extent of the case or any other special circumstance, an additional lay judge over and above what is stated in the first or second sentence shall sit in the court.

If a main hearing is expected to require at least four weeks, the court may consist of two judges learned in law in addition to the panel of lay judges.

In the event of default of a lay judge after commencement of the main hearing the bench is properly constituted with one judge learned in law and a panel of two lay judges or, in cases referred to in the second sentence of the second paragraph, one judge learned in law and a panel of four lay judges.

In a district court a single judge learned in law constitutes the bench

in cases decided without a main hearing,

in all judicial sessions other than main hearings or views of the locus in quo,

at such main hearings in civil actions as are held in simplified form and at other main hearings in civil actions when, in view of the nature of the case, it suffices that the case be decided by a single judge and the parties consent thereto,

at main hearings and views of the locus in quo in criminal cases concerning offences punishable only by fine or imprisonment for at most six months, provided that there is no reason to impose other sanction than a fine. (SFS 1984:131)

**Section 4**

The Government or an authority determined by the Government shall prescribe how many lay judges shall exist in every court district.

After consultation with the lay judges the district court shall assign them to serve in panels. (SFS 1983:370)

**Section 5**

For each district court the Government prescribes the place or places where court shall be held. (SFS 1974:573)

**Section 6**

District courts shall hold sessions as often as required for their business. Sessions for main hearings shall be held at the place prescribed for holding court unless special reasons exist for holding court elsewhere. (SFS 1975:502)

### Section 7

Repealed by SFS 1975:502.

### Section 8

As to special compositions of district courts for hearing of certain cases the specific provisions thereon shall apply. (SFS 1969:244)

### Section 9

In the absence of extraordinary cause, no more cases may be assigned for main hearing on the same day than are likely to be concluded during a period of six hours. When a main hearing cannot be concluded on the day of its commencement, the session shall continue during the required number of consecutive weekdays. If it can occur without inconvenience, however, a recess in the proceedings may take place, so long as the session continues, for a maximum of two or, if there is special cause, three weekdays in one week. (SFS 1969:244)

### Section 10

Repealed by SFS 1975:502.

## Chapter 2

### Courts of Appeals

### Section 1

The courts of appeals have jurisdiction of appeals from the general lower courts. Each court of appeals has supervisory authority over the lower courts within its circuit.

### Section 2

In actions concerning criminal liability or private claim by reason of an offence committed in the exercise of his office or commission by a judge in a general lower court or court-martial or by a judge in bankruptcy, a court registrar or other official directed to handle land registration cases, the courts of appeals function as courts of first instance.

The courts of appeals also sit as courts of first instance in cases concerning which the law so prescribes. (SFS 1974:573)

### Section 3

Each court of appeals shall have a president, one or more division heads and associate judges. They shall be learned in law.

Each court of appeals shall be divided into two or more divisions. Each division shall consist of the president or a division head as the chairman and at least three associate judges, one of whom shall be the deputy chairman.

Each court of appeals shall have a clerical office open to the public at fixed times. (SFS 1969:244)

### Section 4

Three judges learned in law constitute the bench in a court of appeals. In cases appealed from district courts, however, at least four judges learned in law shall sit in the court of appeals if the district court consisted of three or more judges learned in law. No more than five judges learned in law may sit in the court of appeals.

In criminal cases, instead of the provisions in the first paragraph, three judges learned in law and two lay judges constitute the bench in a court of appeals. No more than four judges learned in law and three lay judges may sit in the court. If there is no reason to sentence to a severer sanction than a fine, however, the court is properly constituted also with the composition stated in the first paragraph. The same applies to proceedings outside a main hearing.

For a decision to remove a case from the court's calendar after withdrawal of claim the court of appeals is properly constituted with one judge learned in law.

The extent to which dispositions relating solely to the preparation of a case may be made by a single judge learned in law in the court of appeals or by another officer of the court is prescribed by the Government. (SFS 1984:131)

### Section 4 a

The Government or an authority determined by the Government shall prescribe how many lay judges shall exist in the circuit of the court of appeals to serve in the court of appeals.

After consultation with the lay judges the court of appeals shall assign them to serve in panels. (SFS 1983:370)

### Section 5

Each court of appeals shall hold sessions at the place where it is situated. A court of appeals may also hold sessions at another place, however, if special cause exists therefor.

Sessions shall be held as often as the work of the court requires.

When prescribed by the Government, a court of appeals shall hold sessions annually at fixed times outside its seat at one or more specified places within its circuit for main hearings in cases originating in that part of the circuit. (SFS 1974:573)

#### Section 6

The realm's courts of appeals are: the Svea Court of Appeals, the Göta Court of Appeals, the Court of Appeals for Skåne and Blekinge, the Court of Appeals for Western Sweden, the Court of Appeals for Lower Norrland and the Court of Appeals for Upper Norrland.

The territorial ambit for each of the courts of appeals is prescribed by the Government. (SFS 1974:573)

#### Section 7

Repealed by SFS 1975:502.

## Chapter 3

### Supreme Court

#### Section 1

The Supreme Court has jurisdiction of appeals from the courts of appeals. (SFS 1974:573)

#### Section 2

It is prescribed in chapter 8, section 8, that appeals in specified cases may be brought to the Supreme Court from decisions of the board or other organ of the Association of Advocates. (SFS 1974:573)

#### Section 3

In actions to impose criminal or civil sanctions by reason of an offence committed in the exercise of his office or commission by a cabinet minister, Justice of the Supreme Court, Justice of the Supreme Administrative Court, a Parliamentary Ombudsman, the Attorney General, the Chief State Prosecutor, or anyone who discharges the duties of these officers, or of a judge of a court of appeals, or a law officer of the Supreme Court, the Supreme Court functions as court of first instance.

The Supreme Court shall also as court of first instance determine whether a Justice of the Supreme Court or a Justice of the Supreme

Administrative Court shall be removed from or temporarily suspended from his office or be obliged to submit to medical examination. The Supreme Court also sits as court of first instance whenever this function is specially prescribed. (SFS 1974:573)

**Section 4**

The Supreme Court consists of twenty-two justices or such larger number as, for special cause, is deemed necessary. The justices shall be learned in law. They shall not hold or exercise any other office.

The Government appoints one of the justices chairman of the Court.

The Supreme Court shall work in two or more divisions. The divisions are equally competent to entertain cases over which the Supreme Court possesses jurisdiction.

The Chairman of the Supreme Court is also chairman of a division. The chairman of another division shall be the justice appointed by the Government.

The justices are assigned to the divisions for a specified period according to principles decided by the Supreme Court. (SFS 1974:573)

**Section 5**

During the deliberation concerning a judgment or order, if a division of the Supreme Court finds that the opinion prevailing in the division diverges from a legal principle or construction of law previously adopted by the Supreme Court, the division may direct that the case in its entirety or, if it is feasible, only a certain issue in the case shall be adjudicated by the Supreme Court en banc. Such directive may be given also if otherwise it is of particular importance for judicial application that the case or a certain issue is adjudicated by the Supreme Court en banc.

If, in different judgments or orders known to the division, inconsistent opinions as to a certain legal principle or a certain construction of law have been expressed at different times in the Supreme Court, the rule set forth in the first point in the first paragraph shall be applied only when the division finds that its prevailing opinion diverges from the judgment or order pronounced most recently.

In cases concerning detained persons and in other cases in which expedited adjudication is required by special prescription, the provisions above shall not apply if the case comes before the Supreme Court at a time when it cannot be decided en banc without an injurious prolongation of time.

When a case in decided by the Supreme Court sitting en banc, in the absence of unavoidable impediment all of the justices shall take part in the adjudication. (SFS 1972:147)

### Section 6

Five members of a division of the Supreme Court constitute a quorum. When ruling upon applications for relief for substantive defect or restoration of expired time or limited appeal on account of a grave procedural error three members constitute a quorum if the matter for reviews is of a simple nature. The same applies to review of issues of detention and travel prohibition. Not more than seven members may sit in the court.

Rulings upon requests for dispensation to appeal shall be made by a panel of three justices. If the matter for review is of a simple nature it may be decided by one member. Issues of review dispensation concerning which proceedings have been stayed pursuant to chapter 54, section 11, first paragraph, however, shall be decided by the members who try the case.

A decision to remove a case from the court's calendar after revocation and examination of matters referred to in chapter 55, section 8, second paragraph, first and second sentences, may be made by one member of the division. (SFS 1981:1088)

### Section 7

When a division rules upon an application for relief for substantive defect or limited appeal on account of a grave procedural error in a case adjudicated by the Supreme Court, a member who participated in the earlier adjudication may not serve in the division if a quorum is nevertheless available on the bench. (SFS 1972:147)

### Section 8

For preparation and submission of cases in the Supreme Court there shall be law officers, who shall be learned in law.

The Supreme Court shall have a secretariat. (SFS 1972:147)

## Chapter 4

### Judges

### Section 1

The judges learned in law shall be Swedish citizens and shall have passed the tests of knowledge prescribed for qualification for judgeship.

No person who is legally incompetent or in the state of bankruptcy may discharge the duties of judgeship.

Regulations for tests of knowledge and for conditions in other respects for discharge of the duties of judgeship are issued by the Government. (SFS 1974:573)

**Section 2**

Judges referred to in chapter 1, section 2, chapter 2, section 3, or chapter 3, section 4, shall be nominated by the Government. Law officers of the Supreme Court's secretariat are appointed or designated by the Government. (SFS 1974:573)

**Section 3**

Repealed by SFS 1964:646.

**Section 4**

As to provisions for leave of the judges learned in law of the courts of appeals and the lower courts and the assignment of substitutes in their stead, regulations are prescribed by the Government. (SFS 1974:573)

**Section 5**

The lay judges are elected.

If a court district covers more than one local district, the court divides the number of lay judges among the local districts in proportion to their population, observing that each local district shall elect an even number of lay judges.

The Government or an authority determined by the Government shall prescribe the number of lay judges to be elected to a court of appeals for every county in its circuit or, if its circuit includes part of a county, for that part of the county.

Every third year one half of the number of lay judges in the circuit is elected.

When a lay judge is to be elected, the court must notify the local authority in charge of conducting the election. (SFS 1983:370)

**Section 6**

Any legally competent Swedish citizen who is registered in the local district or, in the case of a lay judge in a court of appeals, in the county or the part thereof which is under the jurisdiction of the court of appeals, and is not more than seventy years of age, is eligible to be a lay judge. Judges learned in law, court officers and employees, public prosecutors, policemen, advocates and all other persons who are professionally engaged in the representation of litigants in judical proceedings, are ineligible for service as lay judges.

No person may be at the same time a lay judge in a court of appeals and in a district court.

No person may refuse designation as a lay judge unless he has attained the age of sixty or establishes a valid excuse on other grounds. A person who has resigned after service as a lay judge is not obliged to serve again during the six years immediately following his period of service.

Examination of the eligibility of the elected person shall be undertaken by the court on its own motion. (SFS 1976:560)

**Section 7**

Election of a lay judge to a district court is undertaken by the local council.

Election of a lay judge to a court of appeals is undertaken by the county council or, if there is in the county a local district not included in a county council region, by the county council and the local council in the proportions decided by the county administrative board on the basis of their populations. In the county of Gotland the election is undertaken by the Gotland local council.

The election shall be proportional if requested by at least the number of electors corresponding to the product resulting when the number of all electors is divided by the number of persons concerned in the election, increased by one. Special regulations exist concerning the procedure for such proportional elections. (SFS 1976:560)

**Section 8**

Lay judges are elected for a period of six years, but they may resign after two years. The court may relieve a lay judge of his obligation to serve even before expiration of the two years period if he establishes a valid excuse. A lay judge who is more than sixty years old may also resign. If a lay judge ceases to meet the eligibility requirements for election, his commission shall expire; a lay judge who has reached the age of seventy years, however, may nonetheless participate in the continued hearing of an action, the processing of which he has attended previously.

If a lay judge resigns during his period of service a new lay judge shall be appointed for the remainder of the period. If the number of lay judges in the court district or county is changed, the person entering upon his duties may be appointed for a shorter period than stated in the first paragraph. (SFS 1976:560)

**Section 9**

A lay judge who has been relieved of his obligation to serve or has resigned, but who is still eligible for election, must continue to fulfil his commission until the court has received notice that another person has been elected in his stead; even thereafter he must serve at the continued hearing of an action, the processing of which he has attended previously.

**Section 10**

When a lay judge is disqualified from participating in a particular case, or fails to attend a session of the court, and no other lay judge can appear without undue delay, the chairman of the court may call as a substitute any person who is eligible for election as a lay judge in the court's territory.

**Section 11**

Each judge shall take the following oath before assuming the duties of his office:

"I N.N. do solemnly swear and assure on my faith and honour that I will and shall impartially administer justice in all matters to the best of my ability and conscience, no less the poor than the rich, and judge according to the law of Sweden's realm; that I will never twist the law or further injustice for kinship, relation by marriage, friendship, envy, ill-will, or fear, nor for bribes and gifts or any other cause, in whatever guise it may appear; nor will I declare guilty one who is innocent, or innocent one who is guilty. Neither before nor after the pronouncement of the court's judgments shall I disclose to the litigants or to other persons the in camera deliberations of the court. All this, as an honest and upright judge, I will and shall faithfully observe."

The oath shall be taken before the court or its chairman. (SFS 1975:1288)

**Section 12**

Those who are or have been married to each other or who are related by blood or marriage in lineal ascent or descent, or who are brothers or sisters, or who are so related by marriage that one of them is or has been married to a brother or sister of the other, or who are similarly related, may not sit together as judges on the bench. (SFS 1973:240)

**Section 13**

A judge shall be disqualified from hearing a case:

1. if he is a party therein or otherwise has an interest in its subject matter or can expect special advantage or injury from the action's outcome;

2. if he and one of the parties are or have been married or are related by blood or marriage in lineal ascent or descent, or are brothers or sisters, or are so related by marriage that one of them is or has been married to a brother or sister of the other, or if he is similarly related to one of the parties;

3. if he is related, as specified in 2, to anyone who has an interest in the subject matter or can expect special advantage or injury from the outcome of the case;

4. if he, or anyone related to him as specified in 2, is a guardian of or otherwise serves as representative of a party, or is a member of the board of a corporation, partnership, co-operative, association or similar society, foundation or similar institution which is a party or, when a municipality or similar community is a party, if he is a member of the board in charge of administration of the subject area within which the case falls;

5. if he, or anyone related to him as specified in 2, is related in the way specified in 4 to anyone who has an interest in the subject matter or can expect special advantage or injury from the outcome of the case;

6. if he is the adversary of a party, though not if the party has cast him in that role in order to disqualify him;

7. if he, acting as a judge or officer of another court, has rendered a decision concerning the matter in controversy or if he, at an authority other than a court or as an arbitrator, has dealt with the matter;

8. if he has served in the case as attorney for or assistant to one of the parties or has been a witness or expert therein; or

9. if some other particular circumstance exists that is likely to undermine confidence in his impartiality in the case. (SFS 1973:240)

**Section 14**

If a judge knows of any circumstance that can be considered to warrant his disqualification, he is obliged to disclose the circumstance.

If a party desires to recuse a judge, he shall raise the objection at his first appearance in court or in his first written submission in the case after notice that the judge sits in the court or is otherwise handling the case or, if at that time the disqualifying circumstance was not known to the party, at his first opportunity to object after he has been apprised of the circumstance. A party who fails to observe this requirement forfeits his right to raise the objection.

The question of disqualification of a judge in a court below may not be entertained in a higher court, unless the objection is made in the higher court by a party who, in accordance with the prescriptions of the second paragraph, is entitled to raise the question, or an appeal is brought against an objection rejected in the court below. (SFS 1983:370)

### Section 15

After the issue of disqualifying a judge has been raised, the judge may act in the case only as to matters that cannot be postponed without extraordinary inconvenience and that are not outcome determinative. Actions of the kind just mentioned may be taken by a judge even if he is declared disqualified.

If a party has moved to disqualify a judge within the prescribed time, the court shall decide the issue separately as soon as possible.

The challenged judge may not take part in the investigation and determination of the issue of his disqualification unless his presence is essential for a properly constituted bench and another judge cannot be called to sit in his place without delay.

## Chapter 5

### Right of Public Attendance and Maintenance of Order at Court Sessions

### Section 1

Court hearings shall be open to the public.

If it can be assumed that at a hearing a declaration may be made which the court must maintain secret in accordance with the Official Secrets Act (1980:100), the court, if it deems it to be of particular importance that the declaration is not disclosed, may direct that the hearing be held behind closed doors insofar as it relates to the declaration. A hearing may be held behind closed doors also in other cases if secrecy must be maintained pursuant to chapter 7, section 22, chapter 8, section 17, or chapter 9, section 15 or 16, of the Official Secrets Act or, with regard to a court hearing during preliminary investigation of a criminal case or equivalent judicial or administrative proceedings, pursuant to chapter 5, section 1, or chapter 9, section 17, of the same Act.

Examination of anyone under the age of fifteen years, or of anyone who is insane or feeble-minded or who suffers from any other mental disturbance, may be held behind closed doors.

Prescriptions stipulated elsewhere permitting closed hearings in specified situations are to be followed. (SFS 1980:101)

**Section 2**

Persons known or appearing to be under the age of twenty-one years may be denied admittance to public hearings when the court's chairman finds it appropriate. (SFS 1974:239)

**Section 3**

The chairman of the court may admit to closed hearings officers of the court and persons who are serving in the court as part of their education. For special cause, the court may also permit other persons to attend such hearings.

**Section 4**

If a hearing has been held behind closed doors and a declaration has been made concerning which the court must maintain secrecy in accordance with the Official Secrets Act (1980:100), the court may direct that the declaration shall not be disclosed. (SFS 1980:101)

**Section 5**

Deliberations on judgments or orders shall occur in camera unless the court finds that they can take place at the bench. When deliberations are held behind closed doors, apart from members of the court, only officers of the court who are involved in the processing of the case may be present. For special cause, however, the court may also permit other persons to be present.

Judgments and orders shall be pronounced in open court. Insofar as the judgment or order contains a declaration concerning which secrecy is ordained in accordance with chapter 12, section 4, second paragraph, of the Official Secrets Act (1980:100), however, the judgment or order shall be pronounced behind closed doors. (SFS 1980:101)

**Section 6**

If a party, a witness or other person who shall be heard by the court is incapable of understanding and speaking Swedish, an interpreter may be called to assist the court.

If an official interpreter for the language in question serves at the court, he shall be called. Otherwise the court shall assign a suitable person to assist it as interpreter in the case.

If the person to be heard has a serious hearing or speech defect, an interpreter may also be called to assist the court.

A person whose interest in the subject matter at issue, or relationship to any of the parties, could be considered to cast doubt on his reliability, may not be called as interpreter.

As to the employment of official interpreters and the calling of an interpreter when the person to be heard has a serious hearing or speech defect, regulations are issued by the Government. (SFS 1975:589)

**Section 7**

Anyone who shall be employed as official interpreter or otherwise assigned to assist as an interpreter shall take on oath before the court that he shall execute the commission assigned to him to the best of his ability. If there is reason to assume that a person assigned to assist as interpreter will receive future commissions as interpreter at the court, he may take an oath relating also to future commissions. (SFS 1975:1288)

**Section 8**

An interpreter is entitled to reasonable compensation for work, loss of time and expenses incurred on the assignment. The tariff to be applied in determining the compensation shall be prescribed by the Government or an authority appointed by the Government. (SFS 1984:131)

**Section 9**

The court's chairman is responsible for the maintenance of order at court hearings and for issuing the directions necessary therefor. He has discretion to expel any person who disturbs a hearing or otherwise behaves in an unseemly manner and, in order to avoid congestion, to limit the number of spectators. The court may forbid any other person to make phonetic recordings of an examination if it may be assumed that the recording will be so embarrassing to the person examined as to be of detriment to the inquiry. The taking of photographs is prohibited in the courtroom.

Expelled persons who force their way into the courtroom or other persons who fail to comply with a directive for the maintenance of order may be arrested and detained on order of the court as long as the hearing lasts, but not for more than three days.

Special regulations exist concerning security control at court proceedings. (SFS 1981:1065)

## Chapter 6

### Court Protocols

#### Section 1

Protocols shall be kept for each case separately.

For proceedings other than hearings a protocol is not required, if

1. the proceeding is conducted by a single judge learned in law or by a court officer,

2. the rulings in the proceeding are separately composed and filed and have been arrived at without difference of opinion in the court, or

3. the case is removed from the court's calendar.

When a judgment in a criminal case at a lower court is rendered in simplified form as stated in chapter 30, section 6, notes may be kept instead of a protocol in accordance with the provisions issued by the Government.(SFS 1982:1123)

#### Section 2

The protocol shall be kept by a court officer, or by a member of the bench learned in law, and signed by him. The chairman himself may keep the protocol when the circumstances so warrant.

A person whose interest in the subject matter at issue or relationship to any of the parties could be considered to cast doubt on his reliability may not be used as protocol keeper. Before acting as protocol keeper, a person who has not taken the oath administered to judges who has not taken the oath administered to judges shall take an oath before the court or its chairman that he shall execute to the best of his ability the duties of protocol keeper and shall not disclose to anyone the court's deliberations in camera. (SFS 1975:1288)

#### Section 3

Each protocol shall contain a record of:

1. the court and the time and place of the hearing;

2. the members of the court, the interpreter, if any, and the protocol keeper;

3. the parties and whether they are present, their attorneys or assistants and, in criminal cases, the defendant's defence counsel;

4. the powers of attorney presented orally before the court;

5. a short description of the subject matter of the case;

6. if a hearing is held behind closed doors, the reason therefor;

7. any decisions of the court that are not separately composed and filed;

8. opinions diverging from the judgment or order.(SFS 1969:244)

**Section 4**

The protocol kept at preparatory hearings shall include:

1. the parties' demands and defences, the amendments thereto and the admissions made on either side;

2. a short statement of the allegations of each party and of the adverse party's reply thereto;

3. the evidence upon which each party seeks to rely and what each item of evidence is intended to prove, as well as specification of the documents and objects offered as evidence; and

4. any other matters deemed necessary in preparation for the main hearing.

If matters required to be noted in accordance with the preceding paragraph are included in party writings or other documents or previously have been noted in the protocols of the case, in lieu of repetition, reference to the documents already on file shall suffice.

The provisions in this section, to the extent relevant, shall apply to protocol keeping at all court proceedings other than the main hearings.

**Section 5**

The protocol kept at main hearings shall summarily state the course of the hearing and include:

1. the parties' demands and defences, the amendments thereto and the admissions made on either side;

2. the demands of persons other than the parties and whether the parties admit or deny them; and

3. the witnesses and experts called for examination and the other items of evidence presented.

If matters required to be noted in accordance with 1 and 2 above are included in party writings or other documents or previously have been noted in a protocol of the case, in lieu of repetition, reference to the documents already on file shall suffice.

## Section 6

Testimony of a witness, an expert, a party under truth affirmation, or an injured person examined in a proceeding brought by a public prosecutor shall be accounted for in the protocol to the extent the testimony can be assumed to be of importance in the action. Observations made by the court at a view of the locus in quo shall also be recorded.

A main hearings in the courts of appeals, the said testimony and observations need not be recorded unless an account thereof can be assumed to become of importance in an appeal to the Supreme Court. At the main hearings in the Supreme Court accounts of testimony and observations are not required.

## Section 7

Statements or events other than those mentioned above may not be recorded at hearings in the absence of special cause therefor. Nor may the legal arguments of the parties be noted in the protocol.

## Section 8

The protocol kept during a hearing shall be finalized before the hearing concludes. When the protocol has been drawn up the chairman shall make a note of its completion thereon.

After testimony which must be noted according to section 6 has been given, the account shall be read out to the examined person or he shall be provided with another opportunity to check it, and thereafter he shall be asked whether or not he has any objection to the account entered. Any objection not resulting in a correction shall be recorded. Thereafter, the account may not be changed. If notes of testimony have not been made directly in the protocol, but the account has been transcribed therein after it has been checked, the original notes shall be attached to the case file.

## Section 9

The court may order that the testimony of parties, injured persons, witnesses or experts, instead of being summarized in the protocol, shall be recorded in shorthand or by phonetic recording. A resumé of the testimony that can be of importance in the action may also be recorded in the same manner.

The provision stated in section 8, second paragraph, of this chapter shall be applied, to the extent relevant, to testimony recorded in shorthand and to resumés of testimony phonetically recorded.

The stenographer is appointed by the court. A person whose interest in the subject matter at issue or relationship to any of the parties can be considered to cast doubt on his reliability may not be used as stenographer. The provisions in chapter 5, section 7, concerning interpreters shall correspondingly be applied to stenographers designated by the court. Stenographers are entitled to reasonable compensation for work, loss of time and expenses incurred. The compensation shall be defrayed out of public funds.

Regulations for rendering into longhand the recordings for which this section provides are issued by the Government. (SFS 1979:289)

#### Section 10

The party writings and other documents in the case, the court's protocols, a copy of the judgment and of any order drawn up separately shall be combined into a case file. Summonses, directions and other orders not noted in a protocol shall also be included in the file by way of a notation on a filed party writing or in another proper way.

The right of the parties and other persons to the return of documents included in the case file is prescribed by the Government. (SFS 1974:573)

#### Section 11

At the court a diary shall be kept, including all cases and stating for each case the time when it was instituted, the procedural steps taken, the date of its determination and, if there was an appeal, the time when the notice of appeal was given or the petition for appeal filed, and the procedural steps taken.

#### Section 12

What has been prescribed in this chapter concerning records, files and diaries in cases must be applied, to the extent appropriate, to non-contentious judicial proceedings.

#### Section 13

Further regulations concerning protocols, files, diaries and other registers are issued by the Government. (SFS 1974:573)

## Chapter 7

### Public Prosecutors and Police Authorities

#### Section 1

The general prosecutors are:

1. the Chief State Prosecutor;
2. the state prosecutors;
3. the district prosecutors.

The duties of the general prosecutors may be performed by assistant prosecutors.

Instructions for the prosecutors are issued by the Government. (SFS 1974:573)

**Section 2**

The Chief State Prosecutor is the supreme prosecutor under the Government and in this capacity is responsible for, and the leader of, the public prosecutors of the realm.

Under the Chief State Prosecutor the state prosecutors, each within his sphere of jurisdiction, are responsible for, and the leaders of, the public prosecutors. (SFS 1974:573)

**Section 3**

The Chief State Prosecutor and the state prosecutors are appointed by the Government. The appointment of other prosecutors is prescribed in the regulations governing their office. (SFS 1974:573)

**Section 4**

The state prosecutors or the district prosecutors are the general prosecutors at the lower courts and the courts of appeals.

The Chief State Prosecutor, however, is the general prosecutor at the courts of appeals in actions referred to in chapter 2, section 2, first paragraph.

The Chief State Prosecutor is the general prosecutor at the Supreme Court.

When a criminal case is appealed to the Supreme Court solely by a private party, the Chief State Prosecutor may assign a subordinate prosecutor to appear on his behalf.

Further regulations concerning the division of work among the prosecutors are stipulated in their instructions. (SFS 1981:1312)

**Section 5**

The Chief State Prosecutor and the state prosecutors may themselves assume an assignment that would otherwise be the responsibility of a subordinate prosecutor. The Chief State Prosecutor and, insofar as the Government decides, the state prosecutors may also appoint a special prosecutor to present a case in the lower courts, in the courts of appeals or, when the appeal is taken solely by a private party, in the Supreme Court.

To the extent prescribed in their instructions, the assistant prosecutors may perform the duties of the public prosecutors whom they assist. Only the Chief State Prosecutor, however, has authority to commence a criminal prosecution or lodge a criminal appeal in the Supreme Court. (SFS 1983:999)

**Section 6**

A circumstance that would disqualify a judge from hearing a particular case also disqualifies a public prosecutor from participating in the preliminary investigation or prosecution of a particular offence. Disqualification of a prosecutor, however, may not be grounded upon an action taken by him in the course of performance of his duty, nor may he be disqualified due to a crime committed against him in, or by reason of, his official capacity.

Although disqualified, a prosecutor may take any measure which cannot be postponed without risk.

The issue of disqualification of a public prosecutor is determined by his immediate superior; the Chief State Prosecutor, however, determines himself the issue of his disqualification. (SFS 1947:616)

**Section 7**

Repealed by SFS 1983:999.

**Section 8**

What is prescribed concerning the exceptional prosecutors shall govern.

No exceptional prosecutor other than the Attorney General or a Parliamentary Ombudsman may institute a criminal prosecution or lodge a criminal appeal in the Supreme Court. (SFS 1968:79)

**Section 9**

The provisions in section 6 concerning public prosecutors are to be correspondingly applied to the police authorities, as also to a policeman who has to take action or notify an order pursuant to this Code; the question of disqualification, however,shall be examined by the police authority. (SFS 1984:388)

## Chapter 8

### Advocates

#### Section 1

There shall be a general association of advocates for the realm. The charter of the association shall be ratified by the Government.

An advocate is one who is a member of the association. (SFS 1974:573)

#### Section 2

Membership of the Association of Advocates is open exclusively to Swedish citizens residing in the realm and at least twenty-five years of age, who have passed the prescribed tests for judgeship qualification and have acquired such practical training and experience as is prescribed in the Association's charter. The applicant shall have made himself known for honesty and in all other respects must be qualified to practise as an advocate.

A person declared incompetent or in the state of bankruptcy may not be accepted for membership.

Judges learned in law, officers and employees at the general courts, public prosecutors and execution officers may not be accepted as members, nor, without special dispensation of the board of the Association of Advocates, may membership be extended to any person employed by the state or a municipality or to a person employed by a private enterprise or individual other than an advocate. The foregoing provisions do not apply, however, to officials at public law offices. (SFS 1972:430)

#### Section 3

Applications for admission to the Association of Advocates are passed upon by its board.

#### Section 4

When practising his profession an advocate shall carry out the tasks entrusted to him honestly and diligently and shall always observe good advocate mores. The obligation of secrecy for advocates at public law offices is prescribed in chapter 9, section 9, of the Official Secrets Act (1980:100). Other advocates are bound, when good advocate mores so require, not to reveal what they learn in the exercise of their profession.

The activities of an advocate may never be carried on in the form of a corporation nor, without special dispensation of the board of the

Association of Advocates, in partnership with any person other than an advocate.

Advocates are obliged to keep segregated from their own property the money and other assets of their clients. (SFS 1980:101)

**Section 5**

Repealed by SFS 1972:430.

**Section 6**

The activities of advocates are supervised by the board of the Association of Advocates. The board shall see to it that the advocates fulfil their duties when pleading and appearing in the courts as well as in their other activities. Advocates are obliged to furnish the board with the information necessary for their board's supervision.

The Attorney General may request the board or, to the extent prescribed by the charter, another organ of the Association, to institute proceedings against an advocate who neglects his duties or who is no longer qualified to remain an advocate.

A person participating in supervisory proceedings at the Association of Advocates shall not improperly disclose what he has learnt in the course thereof concerning anyone's personal or financial circumstances. (SFS 1983:91)

**Section 7**

An advocate deliberately acting incorrectly in his profession, or otherwise acting dishonestly, shall be expelled from the Association. When the circumstances are extenuating, the board may instead give him a warning.

An advocate who in any other respect disregards his professional duties may receive a warning or reminder from the board. When the circumstances are particularly serious, he may be expelled from the Association.

If an advocate is given a warning, he may, for special cause, be ordered to pay a penal charge to the Association, amounting to at least one thousand and at most fifteen thousand crowns.

Matters of expulsion in the cases mentioned above, warning, penal charge or reminder are reviewed by the board of the Association or, to the extent prescribed in the charter, by another organ of the Association. If the review of such matters has been delegated to such an organ, an advocate is under an obligation to deliver to the organ the information needed for its review.

If an advocate ceases to be a Swedish citizen, or if a circumstance occurs that would render him ineligible for membership according to section 2, second or third paragraph, he is bound to resign his membership at once; failing that, the board must expel him. The same applies to an advocate who settles abroad, unless the board consents to continue his membership in the Association.

It may be ordained that a decision to expel anyone from the Association shall take effect forthwith.

A breach of the duty to observe secrecy according to section 4, first paragraph, third sentence, may not be prosecuted by any other than the Attorney General. Prosecution may be brought only if called for on general grounds. (SFS 1982:1114)

### Section 8

Anyone who is denied membership in the Association of Advocates, or who is expelled from it, may appeal from the decision. Appeals from decisions rendered in accordance with section 7 by the organ of the Association authorized to try the matters there mentioned may be brought by the Attorney General.

Such appeals shall be taken to the Supreme Court in the form of limited appeal. (SFS 1963:1491)

## Chapter 9

### On Punishment, Fines and bringing to Court

### Section 1

A party who, against better knowledge, commences, or causes the commencement of, a civil action shall be punished by day-fines.

### Section 2

A party who, against better knowledge, appeals from a judgment or an order shall be punished by day-fines. If the appeal is taken from the judgment or order of a higher court, the punishment shall be fixed at a minimum of twenty-five day-fines.

### Section 3

A party in a civil case, or an injured person in a criminal case, who endeavours to prolong the course of litigation by the interposition of clearly unfounded allegations or defences, by withholding evidence, or by any other improper measure, shall be punished by day-fines. What has been said of a party shall also apply to an intervenor, even if he does not have standing as a party.

**Section 4**

The provisions in sections 1 to 3 shall correspondingly apply to legal representatives, attorneys and assistants.

**Section 5**

Anyone who, at a court session, disturbs the hearing or takes photographs in the courtroom, or fails to obey directions or prohibitions issued by virtue of chapter 5, section 9, shall be punished by fine. The same punishment shall be imposed on anyone who, orally or in a paper filed with the court, expresses himself in an unseemly manner. (SFS 1980:262).

**Section 6**

Anyone who, without adequate excuse, violates a nondisclosure obligation imposed by the court or the investigation authority shall be punished by day-fines.

**Section 7**

If a party or other person should appear in person at a hearing, the court may direct him to do so on penalty of fine. If special provisions concerning directives have been notified, they shall govern.

If a directive which, according to special provisions, shall be accompanied by a fine is served on a person who is resident abroad, the court may refrain from issuing a directive on penalty of fine if service cannot otherwise take place in the foreign state. In the subsequent hearing of the case the directive shall in other respects be regarded as equivalent to a directive to appear on penalty of fine. (SFS 1984:131)

**Section 8**

When parties or other persons are directed to perform or refrain from performing an act on penalty of fine, the court shall fix the fine in an amount which, in view of the addressee's economic situation and other circumstances, can be assumed to be sufficient to induce compliance with the directive. The amount of the fine may not be fixed under ten crowns or above five thousand crowns. If, after the imposition of a fine, the court issues a new directive on penalty of fine, the court may fix the fine at a higher amount, though not exceeding ten thousand crowns. Directives shall be served upon the person named therein.

The provisions in the first paragraph concerning the highest amount of fine do not apply to an order as stated in chapter 15, section 3.

When a specific punishment is prescribed for non-compliance, a conditional fine may not be directed, nor may it be directed against the Crown.

If the reason for which the conditional fine was imposed no longer exists when the issue of final adjudication of the fine comes before the court, the fine shall not be imposed. (SFS 1981:828)

**Section 9**

When according to this Code punishment is by fine, though not day-fine, the lowest fine may be fifty crowns and the highest one thousand crowns. (SFS 1982:1123)

**Section 10**

If a person is to be brought summarily to court, he shall, except as otherwise provided in the sequel, not be taken into custody earlier than is necessary for him to be brought to court directly in time for the session.

If an attempt to bring a person summarily to court has earlier failed or if, by reason of what is known about said person, there is special cause therefor, the court or a police authority may decide that he may be taken into custody earlier than as stated in the first paragraph. Taking into custody may in such case take place at most six hours or, if the decision was made by the court, at most eighteen hours earlier than as stated in the first paragraph. In the court's examination it shall pay particular consideration to the inconveniences that may be assumed to be caused by absence of said person from the hearing before the court.

A person taken into custody in accordance with the second paragraph shall, pending his appearance, remain at the police station or other place determined by the police authority.

A person taken into custody under this clause shall not be subjected to other restriction of liberty than is called for by the purpose of taking into custody, public order or security. (SFS 1984:131)

# Part Two

# Proceedings in General

## I Proceedings in Civil Cases

### Chapter 10

#### Rules of Competence

**Section 1**

The competent court for civil cases in general is the court for the place in which the defendant resides.

When the defendant is registered for census purposes at a place within the realm, that place is deemed to be his residence.

A corporation, partnership, co-operative, association or similar society, foundation or similar institution is considered to reside at the place in which the board has its permanent seat or, if the board has no permanent seat, or there is no board, at the place from which the administration is carried out. The same applies to municipalities or similar communities.

The estate of a deceased person is subject to suit at the place where the deceased would have been required to respond.

A defendant without a known residence either within or outside Sweden is subject to suit at the place where he is sojourning. If he is a Swedish citizen and sojourning outside the realm, or at an unknown place, he may be sued at the place within the realm at which he last resided or sojourned. (SFS 1947:616)

**Section 2**

In civil cases in general, the Crown is subject to suit at the place where the authority charged with representation of the Crown's interest in the subject matter has its seat.

**Section 3**

In controversies concerning debt obligations, anyone without a known residence within the realm may be sued at the place in which property belonging to him is located. In controversies involving personal property, he may be sued at the place at which the property is located.

A debt evidenced by a promissory note, or by any other document the presentation of which is a condition precedent to payment, is deemed to be located where the instrument is kept. Other debt claims are considered to be located in the district in which the debtor resides. If the debt is secured, the place in which the security is kept may also be considered the location of the debt.

**Section 4**

Anyone without a known residence within the realm, who has entered into a contract or otherwise has incurred a debt in the realm, may be sued in a controversy concerning the contract or debt at the place in which the contract was formed or the debt incurred.

**Section 5**

A person engaged in farming, mining, manufacturing, handicraft, commerce, or similar business with a permanent establishment may be sued in a controversy arising directly out of the activity carried on at the establishment at the place in which the establishment is located.

**Section 6**

Anyone who has entered into a contract or otherwise has incurred a debt at a place where he has been residing for a considerable period may be sued with respect to such an obligation at the place of his temporary residence while present at that place. The same rule shall apply to debts incurred for food, lodging and the like at a place of temporary residence.

**Section 7**

Controversies relating to administration by court-appointed guardians and custodians may be instituted at the court in which the guardianship or custodianship is or was last registered, or in the court for the place in which the administration has been performed.

When any other person has administered property belonging to another, controversies relating to that administration may be instituted in the court for the place where the administration has been performed.

**Section 8**

An action for tort damages may be instituted in the court for the place in which the tortious act occurred or had its impact. When the act or its impact occurred at places located in different court districts, the action may be brought in any of these districts.

### Section 9

Controversies concerning the right of succession or the validity of testamentary dispositions or the division of marital property between the decedent's heirs and surviving spouse shall be brought in the court in which the decedent would have been required to respond in civil cases in general.

Controversies concerning divisions of marital property occasioned by a judgment for property division or divorce shall be brought in the court in which the husband is required to respond in civil actions in general or, if the husband is not bound to respond to civil actions generally in any Swedish court, in the court in which the wife is required to respond in such actions.

When in cases referred to in this section no competent court is available, the action shall be instituted in the Stockholm District Court. (SFS 1973:649)

### Section 10

Controversies concerning title to land, or the use and enjoyment of land, or an easement or other special right in land, or possession of land, shall be brought in the court for the place in which the land is situated. The same applies to controversies concerning the liability of an owner or possessor of the land to perform any obligation required of him in this capacity or, when a right to the use of, or other special right in, land has been granted, to controversies concerning consideration for the grant, maintenance of buildings or other similar matters. The provisions of this section do not, however, apply to controversies concerning the rent for leased land or apartments or concerning rights in tenant-owners' apartments.

Controversies by reason of temporary grant of the right to use and enjoyment of land or house or part of a house for placing of vehicles shall, when applying this section, not be considered as leasehold or rent disputes.

When the premises of an estate are located in different court districts, or when a controversy involves more than one estate located in different court districts, the controversy shall be brought in the court of the district in which the main part is located. (SFS 1977:1145)

### Section 11

In the courts mentioned in section 10, the following controversies may also be instituted:

1. controversies concerning the purchase price in a real property sale or other similar claims arising out of the transfer of the ownership of the property;

2. claims against the owner of real estate for personal satisfaction of a debt secured by a mortgage, provided that the personal claim is joined with a claim for satisfaction out of the estate;

3. controversies concerning damage to, or other intrusion upon, land;

4. claims for compensation for work done on real property; and

5. claims for compensation for breach of a covenant of title.

**Section 12**

When applying the rules of this chapter, buildings situated on the land of another, mines, and mine buildings and installations are considered as real property.

**Section 13**

Controversies concerning attorneys' fees and expenses, the division of litigation costs among jointly obligated parties or other persons, and other like claims arising out of litigation may be instituted in the court that originally adjudicated the case.

**Section 14**

Claims based on essentially the same ground against several defendants, when instituted simultaneously, may be brought in the court at which any of the defendants is required to respond under the provisions previously stated in this chapter. Also, if the controversy is such that all interested persons must be bound by the same judgment, the action may be instituted in the court at which any of the defendants is required to respond.

Counterclaims shall be instituted in the court in which the main action is pending.

Claims pursuant to chapter 14, section 4 or 5, shall be instituted in the court in which the main action is pending.

**Section 15**

After the summons has been served upon the defendant, any alteration of the facts determining the court's competence shall be of no legal effect.

**Section 16**

If a written contract stipulates that a controversy already in existence, or one that may arise in the future based upon a legal relationship detailed in the contract, may be instituted in a certain court, or that a certain court exclusively shall be competent, the stipulation is to be complied with unless otherwise stated by law.

**Section 17**

A court is not competent, by reason of the provisions in this chapter, to entertain:

1. controversies assigned to authorities other than the courts, or to the special courts, or required by law or decree to be determined by arbitrators;

2. controversies to be brought in a certain court if, by law or decree, that court is exclusively competent to entertain such controversies;

3. controversies assigned by law exclusively to certain special district courts if the controversy is brought to a court other than the proper one;

4. controversies referred to in section 9 or 10 or which otherwise shall be assigned by law to a court as there stated, if the controversy is brought to a court other than the proper one;

5. marriage cases;

6. controversies concerning attached property or the validity of a contract concerning personal property remaining in the possession of the seller subsequent to sale, as to which special provisions stipulate competent courts; or

7. controversies which can be entertained by the courts without summons.

Nor, by reason of the provisions in this chapter, may an action be instituted in a court at a level other than that prescribed by law for consideration of the controversy; this provision, however, shall not apply to controversies referred to in section 13.

A set-off defence for a money claim may not be entertained by a court which, pursuant to the first paragraph, is not competent to entertain a direct action on the claim asserted by way of set-off. (SFS 1981:828)

**Section 18**

When, pursuant to provisions other than those stated in section 17, a court is incompetent to entertain a controversy instituted in that court, the controversy shall nonetheless be deemed to have been brought in a competent court, unless the defendant has interposed a timely objection to the competence of the court, or has failed to appear in court at the first preparatory hearing or, if the preparation is in writing, to file an answer. If the defendant fails to appear or to file an answer, the plaintiff's statement as to the circumstances that render the court competent shall be accepted as true, provided that the defendant has been notified of the statement, and that there is no reason to believe the statement incorrect.

### Section 19

When a court has entertained a controversy, a higher court may not review the issue of the competence of the court below unless a challenge raised in the court below and rejected there is made the subject of an appeal, or a challenge is raised for the first time in appellate proceedings by a party entitled to do so, or the controversy is of such a nature that it falls within the competence of authorities other than the courts, or of special courts, or the controversy must be instituted originally in a higher court or, by law or decree, must be determined by arbitrators.

### Section 20

When a higher court renders an order that a court below lacked competence to try an action instituted in that court, the higher court, on request of a party, may refer the action to a competent court below.

When more than one court has dismissed an action for lack of competence, and ordinary appellate proceedings are time-barred, the Supreme Court, on application of a party, if it finds any of the courts competent, may refer the action to the court by which the action should have been entertained.

### Section 21

If provisions concerning the competence of courts contained in any law or decree are inconsistent with the regulations contained in this chapter, the former shall govern.

## Chapter 11

### Parties and their Legal Representatives

### Section 1

Any individual can sue or be sued.

When a party does not exercise control of the disputed property, or the dispute involves a legal transaction which the party is not competent to effect, the legal representative of the party shall sue or be sued on his behalf. As to actions based on tortious acts, the provisions in chapter 20, section 14, and chapter 21, section 1, first paragraph, shall correspondingly apply.

**Section 2**

Any corporation, partnership, co-operative, association or similar society, foundation or similar institution, which can acquire substantive rights and assume legal liabilities can sue or be sued. The same applies to the Crown, the municipalities and similar communities.

The authority to present the claims and defences of such parties resides in their legal representatives. (SFS 1947:616)

**Section 3**

Any foreigner who is incompetent to sue or be sued by the law of his homeland is nevertheless entitled to sue or be sued in the courts of the realm if competent according to Swedish law.

**Section 4**

It is not necessary to prove the capacity of a party to sue or be sued, or the authority of an individual to sue or be sued as a party on his own behalf or as a legal representative of a party, unless the court directs otherwise.

**Section 5**

At the main hearing in a lower court or in a court of appeals, a party shall attend in person, unless his presence can be assumed to lack importance for the investigation. At the main hearing in the Supreme Court a party has the duty to attend in person, if his presence is found necessary for the investigation. At a preparatory hearing in a lower court a party shall also attend in person, if it can be assumed that the preparation will be promoted thereby. At hearings other than those mentioned, a party is bound to attend in person, if it is found necessary.

These provisions as to the obligation of parties to attend in person shall also apply to their legal representatives. If a party has more than one legal representative, the court may direct one or more of the authorized persons to appear in person. Even if an individual lacks the capacity to sue or be sued on his own behalf, he is nevertheless obliged to attend in person, if his presence is found necessary for the investigation.

When a party or a legal representative is required to appear in person, the court shall notify him to attend.

## Chapter 12

### Attorneys in Litigation

#### Section 1

The parties may present their cases by attorney.

The duty of a party to appear in person is prescribed in chapter 11, section 5.

#### Section 2

Only a person deemed suitable by the court to be an attorney in the case with regard to his honesty, knowledge and earlier activities may appear as an attorney.

An attorney shall be a Swedish citizen residing in the realm; however, the court may permit a person who does not meet these qualifications to serve as attorney for a party if, with regard to the nature of the case and other circumstances, such permission is found appropriate.

A minor, or a person declared incompetent or in the state of bankruptcy, may not appear as an attorney. (SFS 1956:230)

#### Section 3

Judges and officers learned in law employed in the general courts, public prosecutors and execution officers may not appear as attorneys unless the Government or an authority determined by the Government grants an exception for a particular case. This prohibition shall not apply, however, to a person who, while on leave of absence and for educational purposes, works as assistant to an advocate.

No lay judge may appear as attorney in the court of which he is a member. (SFS 1975:1288)

#### Section 4

No one related as specified in chapter 4, section 12, to a judge who is a member of the judicial panel processing a case may appear in that case as an attorney. Nor may anyone appear who has had a prior connection with the subject matter as a judge or court officer, or as an attorney for the adverse party.

#### Section 5

When an attorney is shown to be dishonest, lacking in skill, or imprudent, or is otherwise deemed unsuitable, the court shall dismiss him as an attorney in the case; for cause, the court may also declare him to be incompetent to act as an attorney before it either for a certain period or until further notice.

### Section 6

When a court dismisses an attorney, unless the party is present and desires to appear pro se, the court shall direct the party to commission a suitable attorney. If the party fails to do so and does not appear in person, he shall be deemed in default.

If the dismissed attorney is an advocate, the court shall notify the board of the Association of Advocates of his dismissal.

### Section 7

If anyone who may not appear as an attorney seeks as a party to recover upon an assigned claim, and it is found probable that the claim was transferred to him in order to make it possible for him to appear pro se, the court shall direct him to commission an attorney. If the party fails to do so, he shall be deemed in default.

### Section 8

A party desiring to be represented by an attorney shall give the attorney a power of attorney either orally before the court or in writing. A power of attorney in writing shall be signed by the party in his own hand.

### Section 9

A written power of attorney shall be presented to the court in the original at the first occasion on which the attorney acts on behalf of the party.

If the power of attorney is not available at the prescribed time, the court, except with respect to notices of appeal and of exceptions to court rulings, shall give the attorney time to produce it. If a postponement is deemed inconvenient, the court may continue the proceedings, except that it may not pronounce its judgment or final order. If a power of attorney is issued, the power shall be deemed to authorize the acts previously performed in the proceedings by the attorney on behalf of the party.

If the court doubts the signature of a party on the power of attorney, it may grant a postponement pending removal of the doubt.

Either the original or a certified copy of a power of attorney shall be filed in the case file.

### Section 10

When, pursuant to specially issued provisions, the content of a written power of attorney has been communicated by telegraph or telephone, the note of the communication is valid as power of attorney. If the court finds it necessary, however, the power of attorney shall be presented in the original; upon non-compliance with an order to this effect the note of the communication will be deemed invalid.

Further regulations concerning the communication of powers of attorney are issued by the Government. (SFS 1974:573)

**Section 11**

Where the Crown, a municipality or other similar community, or a public institution is concerned, a commission duly executed, or an extract from the report of a resolution appointing the attorney, is valid as a power of attorney. With regard to a corporation, partnership, co-operative, association or similar society, or a foundation or similar institution, a certified copy from the report of such a resolution appointing the attorney is valid as a power of attorney. (SFS 1947:616)

**Section 12**

A power of attorney shall state the name of the attorney. It may not be addressed to the bearer.

A power of attorney shall refer to a certain case, or to judicial proceedings in general. If a party wishes to issue a power of attorney limiting representation to a certain court, or a particular hearing, the party shall so state in the power. A power of attorney presented orally before the court is valid only in the case in which it has been presented.

**Section 13**

In the absence of consent of the party, an attorney may not delegate his responsibilities to another representative.

If an attorney has the right to delegate, his substitute may also delegate his responsibilities to another, provided that the original attorney has given his consent to such further delegation.

**Section 14**

A power of attorney authorizes the attorney on behalf of the party:

1. to institute an action and to apply for other relief, even if such relief must be sought from an authority other than the court;

2. to be served with party writings and other documents, except notices for attendance of the party in person;

3. to perform all acts relating to presentation of the party's claims, and to present the defence to each claim asserted against the party;

4. to withdraw a claim made by the party, and to consent to a claim made by the adverse party;

5. to settle the action;

6. to apply for execution of the court's judgment; and

7. to collect litigation costs awarded to the party.

A power of attorney to conduct judicial proceedings in general does not authorize the attorney to institute an action on a claim not amenable to out of court settlement, nor to be served with the summons in such an action.

A power of attorney limited to as certain court authorizes the attorney as specified in the first paragraph; the attorney may also take exception to court rulings and present a notice of appeal from a judgment rendered by the court.

A power limited to a certain hearing authorizes the attorney as specified in the first paragraph 2–5; the attorney may also notify the court of exceptions to its rulings and present a notice of appeal from a judgment rendered at that hearing.

**Section 15**

The authority of an attorney pursuant to section 14 may be restricted only as to his power to institute an action, to be served with the summons, to settle an action, to apply for execution of the court's judgment, or to collect the litigation costs awarded to the party; any other restriction upon his authority shall be void.

A permitted restriction of the power of attorney made after issuance of the power is not effective with respect to the court and the adverse party until the restriction has been brought to their knowledge either orally before the court or in writing.

**Section 16**

When a power of attorney is not composed as required by section 12, the court shall direct the party to correct the error. Failure to do so renders the power of attorney void.

**Section 17**

Any act by the attorney in the course of the litigation done in the presence of the party is ineffective as to the latter if he immediately protests against the act.

**Section 18**

A power of attorney can be terminated by the party at any time.

An attorney desiring to resign from his commission has the duty to protect the interests of the party according to the power of attorney until the party has had an opportunity to make other arrangements for the conduct of his case.

The termination or relinquishment of a power of attorney is not effective with respect to the court and the adverse party until it has been brought to their knowledge either orally before the court or in writing.

**Section 19**

If the party dies or loses the right to dispose of the subject matter involved in the dispute, the power of attorney does not cease to be valid. However, if cause therefor exists, the court shall notify the heirs of the deceased party, or his legal representative, of the action.

If a power of attorney has been issued by the legal representative of a party and thereafter the representative loses his authority, the power of attorney remains valid.

**Section 20**

Anyone acting as an attorney is accountable for his authority to act in that capacity and, when unable to prove that he has acted according to a power of attorney, or that an act done by him in the course of the action has been ratified by the party or is otherwise binding upon the party, he is obliged to compensate the adverse party or another for the costs accruing in the action by reason of those of his acts which were not binding upon his party. As to liability to compensate for other damages, the provisions concerning powers of attorney in general shall correspondingly apply.

**Section 21**

The provisions in this chapter concerning an attorney authorized to present a case on behalf of a party shall apply, to the extent appropriate, to an attorney authorized to perform a particular act in the course of a proceeding.

**Section 22**

Although appearing pro se, a party may commission an assistant. The provisions in sections 2 to 5 and section 6, second paragraph, shall apply to such an assistant. Any act done in the course of the action by the assistant in the presence of the party shall be deemed authorized by the latter unless he immediately protests against the act.

### Section 23

Any agent who manages property or other economic interests for his principal under a general power, and is authorized also to present cases concerning the property or interests on behalf of his principal, shall have standing as a legal representative.

### Section 24

Wherever there is a special provision in a law or decree concerning the authority to present a case on behalf of another person, that provision shall govern.

## Chapter 13

### Justiciable Controversies; Commencement of Actions

### Section 1

A claim for judgment directing the defendant to perform a specified act or series of acts may be adjudicated upon the merits, although the claim does not fall due prior to the completion of the action, provided that

1. the claim is for periodic payments, and either does not depend upon the performance of a past or future reciprocal obligation, or is in the form of a pension or an annuity owed by reason of a reciprocal obligation already performed, and that at least one of the payments is due;

2. the claim will fall due immediately upon default of a primary obligation which constitutes the principal claim in the case;

3. the claim is for interest pending payment of a mature debt or for other auxiliary obligations arising from the principal obligation;

4. it is important for the plaintiff that the claim be discharged within the agreed time, and there is reason to believe that the defendant will disregard his undertaking; or

5. the institution of such a claim is otherwise authorized by law.

### Section 2

A claim for a judgment declaring whether or not a certain legal relationship exists may be adjudicated upon the merits if an uncertainty exists as to the legal relationship, and the uncertainty exposes the plaintiff to a detriment.

If determination of a performance claim depends upon whether or not a certain disputed legal relationship exists, a claim for a declaratory judgment as to the relationship may be entertained.

Whenever claims for declaratory judgments are authorized by other laws, the provisions of such laws shall govern.

### Section 3

The claim presented in the summon application may not be amended. However, the plaintiff may:

1. by reason of a circumstance that occurred or became known to him during the proceeding, demand a performance other than that initially requested;

2. request a declaratory judgment pursuant to section 2, second paragraph; and

3. claim interest or other auxiliary obligations arising from the principal obligation, and also assert an additional claim supported upon essentially the same ground as the original claim.

Claims pursuant to 2 or 3 raised after the main hearing has commenced may be dismissed without reaching the merits, if their adjudication cannot occur without inconvenience. Nor may such additional claims be presented for the first time in appellate proceedings.

The plaintiff's reduction of his claim or, without changing the original subject matter, his allegation of new circumstances in support of his claim, does not constitute an amendment.

### Section 4

An action shall be initiated by summons, unless otherwise prescribed.

A plaintiff desiring to amend his claim as authorized by section 3 may do so orally before the court or in writing. The defendant shall be notified of the amendment.

An action shall be deemed initiated when the summons application is filed with the court or, if a summons is not necessary, when the claim is presented to the court.

### Section 5

In cases amenable to out of court settlement, if the plaintiff withdraws his claim after the defendant has responded, the action shall nonetheless be adjudicated if the defendant so requests.

In cases other than those mentioned in the first paragraph, if the plaintiff withdraws his claim after the entry of the judgment and without the consent of the defendant, the withdrawal is without effect.

### Section 6

While an action is pending, a new action involving the same subject matter between the same parties may not be entertained.

### Section 7

If the plaintiff transfers the disputed matter, the transferee has the right, without a new summons, to take over the claim in the action in the shape it has at the time of his admission in the proceeding. The liability of the transferor for litigation costs is prescribed in chapter 18, section 10.

If a transfer occurs on the defendant's side, the transferee, upon the consent of the plaintiff, may be substituted for the original defendant.

In the event of a transfer of the disputed matter by either the plaintiff or the defendant, on the application of the adverse party the transferee is obliged to join as a party in the action.

## Chapter 14

### Joinder of Parties and Claims; Joinder of third Parties

### Section 1

Claims instituted by a plaintiff at the same time against the same defendant shall be joined in a single action if they are supported on essentially the same ground.

### Section 2

When claims have been instituted at the same time by a plaintiff against more than one defendant, or by more than one plaintiff against one or more defendants, the claims shall be joined in a single action if they are supported on essentially the same ground.

### Section 3

If the defendant requests joint processing with the plaintiff's claim of a claim instituted by the defendant against the plaintiff concerning the same or a related subject matter, or of a debt that may be set-off against the plaintiff's claim, and his request is presented prior to the commencement of the main hearing, the claims shall be joined in a single action. A claim thus joined with the main claim is a counterclaim.

**Section 4**

If anyone who is not a party to the original action requests joint processing when instituting a claim against both of the original parties, or one of them, concerning the disputed matter, and his request is presented prior to the commencement of the main hearing, the claims shall be joined in a single action.

**Section 5**

If a party, in the event that a judgment should be entered against him, wishes to present a claim for resession, indemnification or the like against a third party, he may, prior to the commencement of the main hearing, institute his claim against the third party for joint processing with the pending action. This rule shall correspondingly apply if a third party, in consequence of the outcome of a pending action, wishes to institute such a claim against one or both of the parties. (SFS 1970:1002)

**Section 6**

Claims between the same or different parties may also be joined in a single action in situations other than those described above if it is of advantage to the investigation. For cause, the claims may later be served and processed separately.

**Section 7**

The provisions of sections 1 to 6 authorizing joinder of claims in a single action apply only when the claims have been instituted in the same court, and that court is competent to try the claims, and the same rules of procedure apply to each.

**Section 8**

If there is more than one plaintiff or defendant, each of them is treated as an independent party against the adverse party or parties.

When the nature of the disputed matter requires that all interested parties be bound by the same judgment, any procedural act of one of the co-parties operates to the advantage of all of them, even if the act was contrary to acts of other co-parties.

**Section 9**

Anyone not a party to a pending action who states that the disputed matter is related to his legal right or obligation, and who shows probable cause for his statement, may appear as an intervenor in the action on the side of either the plaintiff or the defendant.

### Section 10

A person desiring to intervene in a pending action shall make an application therefor to the court. The parties shall be given notice of, and an opportunity to respond to, the application. For cause, the court may order a hearing on the application attended by the parties and the applicant. The court shall render its decision whether or not to grant leave to intervene as soon as possible.

### Section 11

An intervenor may take any procedural act open to the party whom he supports; he may not, however, amend the party's claim, or otherwise act in opposition to the party, or appeal from a judgment or order except by supporting the appeal of the party.

When, however, by reason of the nature of the legal situation or otherwise, the intervenor will be bound by the judgment issued in the action to the same extent as if he had been an original party thereto, he has full party standing therein.

### Section 12

Any party who considers that a third person is entitled to intervene in the action may notify the third person and request that he appear in the proceeding.

A person so notified may in turn notify another person whom he considers to be entitled to intervene in the action.

As to the obligation of a party in certain situations to notify a third person of an action, special provisions have been enacted.

### Section 13

Notice of an action is given by service of a written declaration. The declaration shall also be served upon the adverse party. The declaration shall state the matter in dispute and the reason for the notice.

## Chapter 15

### Provisional Attachment, Injunction against Dissipation, and other Security Measures.
### Interlocutory Decrees

### Section 1

If a person has shown probable grounds for possession of a claim which is or may be presumed to be the subject of legal proceedings or adjudication in other similar form, and it can reasonably be expected that the adverse party, by absconding, removal of property or by other means, will evade payment of the debt, a court may order provisional attachment of so much of the adversary's property that the claim may be assumed to be covered in the event of distraint. (SFS 1981:828)

**Section 2**

If a person has shown probable grounds for having a superior right to certain property which is or may be presumed to be the subject of legal proceedings or adjudication in other similar form, and it can reasonably be expected that the adverse party will remove, essentially impair or otherwise take possession of the property to the detriment of the applicant, a court may order provisional attachment of the property. (SFS 1981:828)

**Section 3**

If a person, in a case other than referred to in section 1 or 2, shows probable grounds for possession of a claim against any other which is or may be presumed to be the subject of legal proceedings or adjudication in other similar form, and it can reasonably be expected that the adverse party, by carrying on a certain activity or performing or refraining from performing a certain act, or by other means will prevent or render difficult the exercise of the claimant's right or substantially diminish its value, a court may impose an appropriate sanction to secure the claimant's legal right.

A sanction as stated in the first paragraph may entail prohibition, on penalty of fine, to carry out a certain activity or perform a certain act or an order, on penalty of fine, to respect the claimant's title, or appointment of a custodian, or the issue of directions otherwise calculated to prevent encroachment upon the claimant's legal right. (SFS 1981:828)

**Section 4**

In an action concerning superior right to property, if it is apparent that one party has unlawfully infringed the adverse party's possession or taken any other unlawful action in respect of the property, the court may direct that the possession be immediately restored or other rectification immediately made. (SFS 1981:828)

**Section 5**

Orders concerning the measures authorized by this chapter are issued by the court in which the action is pending. If an action is not pending, the question of competency of the court shall be governed by the directions for civil actions. The stipulations concerning restriction of a court's competency in respect of a controversy to be adjudicated otherwise than before a court shall, however, not apply.

The question of imposition of a measure as stated in this chapter may be determined only on request. If an action is not pending, the request shall be made in writing.

A request may not be granted unless an opportunity to respond thereto has been given to the adverse party. When delay entails risks, however, the court may act immediately, issuing an order which remains effective until it directs otherwise.

As regards the hearing in other respects of a question concerning a measure authorized in section 1, 2 or 3 when an action is not pending, the procedure shall be that applying when such a question arises in an action. A request by the claimant's adverse party for remuneration of costs may, however, be considered in conjunction with the decision concerning the question of the measure to be imposed. (SFS 1981:828)

**Section 6**

A measure authorized in section 1, 2 or 3 may be granted only if the claimant deposits with the court security to recompense the adverse party for the loss he may suffer. A claimant who is unable to furnish security may be excused by the court if he shows that his claim has extraordinary merit. The State, local and regional authorities need not furnish security.

As to the nature of security, the provisions in chapter 2, section 25, of the Code of Execution shall apply. The security shall be determined by the court if not assented to by the adverse party. (SFS 1981:828)

**Section 7**

When a measure authorized in section 1, 2 or 3 has been granted, if an action has not already been brought, the claimant shall, within one month of the order, bring an action before a court or, if the claim is to be entertained in another form, in accordance with the provisions pertaining thereto. An action that is not to be entertained by a court or other authority shall be considered to have been brought when a request for examination has been addressed to the adverse party or the procedure has been initiated by other means.

If an action is not brought as stated in the first paragraph, the measure shall be immediately rescinded. (SFS 1981:828)

**Section 8**

A measure granted in accordance with section 1, 2 or 3 shall be immediately terminated if security relating to the purpose of the measure is furnished or there is otherwise no longer any reason for the measure. If a claim is withdrawn or dismissed without reaching the merits, the measure shall also be immediately terminated.

The question of termination is determined by the court in which the action is pending or, if no action is pending, by the court which first dealt with the issue.

When finally adjudicating a case brought to trial the court shall determine whether the measure shall continue in effect. A measure as stated above may also be ordered by the court in conjunction with its final judgment in the case. (SFS 1981:828)

### Section 9

On the request of either party, for cause, the court may rescind an order imposed under section 4. (SFS 1981:828)

### Section 10

As to execution of a measure authorized by this chapter the provisions of the Code of Execution shall apply. The court may issue further directions concerning execution if so required. (SFS 1981:828)

# Chapter 16

## Voting

### Section 1

In the deliberation on a judgment or order, if there are diverging opinions, voting shall take place.

Opinions shall be declared by the judges in reverse order of their length of service except that, regardless of seniority, the court's chairman votes last. When a judge of the panel has presided at the preparation of the case, he states his opinion first.

Each member of a court shall state the grounds upon which he rests his opinion. (SFS 1969:244)

### Section 2

The court shall vote separately upon procedural issues.

If there are several claims in an action, the court shall vote separately upon each claim. It shall also vote separately on a debt asserted as a set-off defence. If there are separate issues of fact, each of which may bear directly upon the outcome of a claim, such issues shall be posed for separate voting to the extent required by the nature of the matter in controversy. The court shall vote separately on the assessment of litigation costs.

A member of the court who has been outvoted on a particular issue is obliged to participate in subsequent voting, accepting as a premise thereof the position of the majority on the issue as to which he dissented.

**Section 3**

The vote of the majority shall prevail. In the event of a tie the chairman's vote is decisive. (SFS 1971:218)

**Section 4**

If there are more than two opinions, none of which controls pursuant to section 3, and the issue concerns a monetary demand or any other quantitative demand for relief, the votes for the highest amount shall be counted with the votes for the next highest amount and, if necessary, the counting shall continue on the same basis until a determination with the required support is reached; otherwise the opinion obtaining the most votes or, when two or more opinions have an equal number of votes, the opinion supported by the most prominent member among those voting for one of these opinions shall prevail. (SFS 1969:244)

**Section 5**

If there is a disagreement about how voting shall proceed, or which opinion shall prevail, the disagreement shall be resolved by voting.

**Section 6**

When a question of criminal responsibility, final adjudication of a conditional fine or detention of a person is presented in a civil case, the voting provisions of chapter 29 shall apply thereto. (SFS 1981:828).

**Section 7**

Repealed by SFS 1969:244.

## Chapter 17

### Judgments and Orders

#### Section 1

The final determination of an action upon the merits by a court is a judgment. Any other decision in an action by a court is an order. An order finally servering an action from the court otherwise than by a judgment is a final order. An order rendered by a higher court upon an issue separately appealed to that court also constitutes a final order.

#### Section 2

If the court has held a main hearing, the judgment shall be based upon material presented at that hearing. A judge may not participate in the judgment unless present throughout the main hearing. If a new main hearing has been held, the judgment shall be based upon material presented at that hearing.

When an action is adjudicated without a main hearing, the judgment shall be based upon the contents of the documents and anything else that has occurred in the action.

#### Section 3

A judgment may not grant different or more extensive relief than has been properly demanded by a party. In cases amenable to out of court settlement, the judgment may not be based upon circumstances not alleged by a party as the foundation of his cause.

#### Section 4

When several claims amenable to severance are joined in a single action, the court may enter a judgment upon any of the claims separately, although the processing of the remaining claims has not been terminated. However, a main debt claim and a debt asserted by the defendant by way of set-off must be adjudicated simultaneously. When a defendant concedes a part of a single claim, a separate judgment may be entered as to that part.

#### Section 5

In an action involving both a claim for a declaration as to the existence of a specified legal relationship and a claim for performance based upon the existence of that legal relationship, a separate judgment may be entered upon the declaratory claim. In any other situation in which the adjudication of a certain claim depends upon the outcome of another claim joined in the same action, a separate judgment may be rendered as to the threshold claim.

If, in respect of the same claim, there are several circumstances, each of which are of direct significance for the outcome, and if separate adjudication is found to be appropriate in view of the nature of the inquiry, on request of a party a separate judgment may be rendered thereon; against the objection of a party such a judgment may not be rendered in the absence of extraordinary cause therefor.

When rendering a separate judgment pursuant to this section, the court may order a stay of proceedings upon the remaining issues in the case pending conclusiveness of the separate judgment. (SFS 1971:218)

**Section 6**

If the parties agree upon a settlement of the disputed matter, and they both request it, the court shall confirm their settlement agreement by judgment.

**Section 7**

A judgment shall be in writing and specify in separate sections:

1. the court, time and place of pronouncement of the judgment;

2. the parties and their attorneys or assistants;

3. the ultimate order of the court;

4. the parties' demands and defences and the circumstances upon which they are founded; and

5. the reasoning in support of the judgment, including a statement of what has been proved in the action.

A judgment rendered by an appellate court shall, to the necessary extent, describe the judgment of the lower court.

If a party may appeal from a judgment or apply for the reopening of a default judgment, the judgment shall state the steps he must take to do so. Further instructions to be included in a judgment of a court of appeals are prescribed in chapter 54, section 14. (SFS 1976:567)

**Section 8**

A default judgment, a judgment granting the claim of the plaintiff with the defendant's consent, and a judgment by an appellate court confirming the judgment of a lower court, may be rendered in simplified form. (SFS 1976:567)

**Section 9**

Before rendering judgment the court shall meet to deliberate.

When a main hearing has been held, deliberation shall take place either on the same day or on the next working weekday and, if possible, the judgment shall be determined and read out in open court prior to adjournment. When the nature of the case is such that a considerable period of time is required for the determination and composition of the judgment, the court may defer its pronouncement. However, unless there is an extraordinary obstacle, the judgment shall be composed in writing and pronounced within two weeks of conclusion of the main hearing. If the judgment is not read out in open court at the main hearing, it shall be read at another session of the court or be held accessible to the public at the courts's clerical office; at the conclusion of the main hearing the court shall notify the parties of the time and manner of the pronouncement of judgment.

The rules stated above in this section shall also apply to actions finally adjudicated at a preparatory hearing.

In actions which are adjudicated without a main hearing the deliberation shall take place and the judgment be determined, composed in writing and pronounced as soon as possible. Pronouncement shall occur by making the judgment accessible at the court's clerical office. A notice of the time of the pronouncement shall be sent to the parties, at the latest, on the same day as the pronouncement.

Pronouncement of a judgment in open court may occur by reporting the reasoning in support of the judgment and the ultimate order and by notifying the parties concerning the means by which the judgment may be attacked.

If a divergent opinion has been expressed, it shall be notified to the parties at the same time and in the same manner as the judgment.

When the action has been adjudicated, the parties shall be notified in writing of the outcome as soon as possible. (SFS 1976:576)

**Section 10**

Every judgment shall be separately drawn up and signed by each of the judges learned in law participating in the adjudication.

All the judgments rendered by a court during a calendar year, filed and numbered consecutively by date of issuance, shall be put together to compose a judgment book.

**Section 11**

Upon the expiration of the time for ordinary means of attack, a judgment acquires binding force in so far as it decides the particular matter concerning which the claim was instituted.

A judgment also has binding force to the extent that it adjudicates a debt obligation claimed as a set-off.

Nor may a question thus decided be taken up again for adjudication.

As to extraordinary means of attack, the specific provisions thereon shall apply.

**Section 12**

The provisions of section 2 and 9 concerning judgments shall correspondingly apply to final orders. If the nature of the matter so requires, the provisions in sections 7 and 10 shall also apply to such orders. When a final order is rendered in an action in conjunction with a judgment, the final order shall be included in the judgment.

If a party may appeal from a final order or apply for reinstatement, the order shall provide instructions as to the steps he must take to do so. Further instructions to be included in a final order of a court of appeals are prescribed in chapter 54, section 14.

**Section 13**

An order other than a final order shall state, to the extent necessary, the reasoning supporting the determination.

If a person who desires to appeal from an order rendering during the processing of an action must take formal exception thereto, the court shall instruct him to that effect. In an appeal from such an order must be brought independently, the court shall also instruct the parties thereon. Any party desiring to appeal from the order may request of the court further instructions concerning the taking of an appeal.

When an order other than a final order is rendered in an action in conjunction with a judgment or final order, the order shall be included in the judgment or final order. If an appeal from the order must be brought independently, the court shall furnish instructions as to the steps necessary to perfect an appeal.

Further instructions to be included in the order of a court of appeals are prescribed in chapter 54, section 14.

**Section 14**

For cause, the court may direct in the judgment that it may be subject to immediate execution. When reason exists, the court shall prescribe that security shall be furnished for damages which the party may be liable to pay if the judgment is amended.

Orders rendered during the proceedings which may not be challenged separately shall be immediately effective. The same applies to orders by which the court:

1. has dismissed an attorney or assistant,

2. denied a third party's application to intervene in an action,

3. decided the compensation or advance payment to an assistant, witness, expert, or any other person who is neither a party nor an intervenor,

4. directed that a person be held in custody or ordered provisional attachment or other security measure as stated in chapter 15 or the dissolution of such measure,

5. has appointed as assistant a person other than the one proposed by the party, or

6. given a ruling in a case other than referred to in 3 or 5 on a matter relating to public legal aid, but not a decision concerning obligation to indemnify as stated in section 31 of the Legal Aid Act (1972:429).

In respect of an order directing a party or third person to produce a document or make accessible an object for view or inspection the provisions of the first paragraph shall apply.

Any special provision prescribing that a judgment or order be subject to immediate execution shall govern. (SFS 1981:828)

### Section 15

When the court finds as the result of a complaint or otherwise that a judgment or order is evidently incorrect owing to an error in transcription, calculation or any other similar oversight, after affording the parties an opportunity to be heard it shall direct amendment of the judgment or order.

An amendment shall be entered directly upon the original judgment or order or, if the order is included in a protocol, upon the protocol and, if possible, upon all copies of the judgment or order, together with a notation of the date of the entry.

## Chapter 18

### Litigation Costs

### Section 1

The losing party shall reimburse his adversary for litigation expenses if nothing to the contrary is provided.

**Section 2**

In an action concerning a matter that by law may not be resolved finally without judicial confirmation, the court may direct that each party shall bear his own expenses.

**Section 3**

If the winning party is found to have initiated the action without provocation from his adversary, or otherwise to have deliberately or negligently caused unnecessary litigation, he shall reimburse his adversary for the latter's, litigation expenses, or, if the circumstances so justify, each party shall bear his own expenses.

If the losing party neither knew nor should have known of the outcome determinative circumstances prior to the commencement of the action, the court may direct that each party shall bear his own expenses.

**Section 4**

If in a multi-claim action each party is both winner and loser, either each party shall be required to bear his own expenses, or one of the parties shall be awarded an adjusted compensation for his expenses, or, to the extent that the expenses attributable to different parts of the action are severable, the liability to compensate for expenses shall be determined by the outcome of each part. However, if the portion of the case which the party has lost is of only minor importance, he may receive full compensation for his expenses.

If only a part of a party's claim is granted, the preceding paragraph shall correspondingly apply.

**Section 5**

A party whose claim is dismissed without reaching the merits is deemed the loser.

A party who withdraws his claim or whose claim is written off by reason of his failure to appear shall reimburse the adverse party for his expenses, unless special circumstances indicate that a different resolution is appropriate.

If the parties settle the action by private agreement, in the absence of a contrary provision in the settlement agreement, each party shall bear his own expenses.

**Section 6**

If a party's failure to appear or to comply with a court direction, or presentation of a claim or defence that he knew or should have known to be without merit, or carelessness or oversight in other respects has occasioned adjournment of the proceedings or has otherwise caused expenses for the adverse party, that party must reimburse the adverse party for such expenses, regardless of how costs in general are to be distributed.

**Section 7**

If, pursuant to this chapter, a party must provide compensation for the adverse party's litigation expenses, in whole or in part, and it is found that the party's legal representative, attorney or assistant has caused the expenses by conduct described in section 3, first paragraph, or by such carelessness or oversight as is referred to in section 6, the court, even if not requested to do so, may impose joint liability for costs upon the party and his representative, attorney or assistant.

**Section 8**

Compensation for litigation expenses shall fully cover the expenses of preparation and presentation of the action including counsel fees to the extent that the expenses were reasonably incurred for the protection of the party's interest. Compensation shall also be paid for the time and effort expended by the party by reason of the action. As measure for preparation of the action is considered a hearing for settling an issue at dispute that is of direct significance for the party's suit.

Compensation for litigation expenses shall also include interest at six per cent from the date of adjudication of the action until payment is made. (SFS 1981:741)

**Section 9**

If compensation for litigation expenses is to be furnished by several parties joined on the same side, such parties are jointly and severally liable for the expenses. However, to the extent that items of expense are chargeable to a portion of the action involving only one of the co-parties, or that one of the co-parties has occasioned items of expense by such carelessness and oversight as is described in section 6, only he co-party who occasioned the expenses shall be charged.

When, pursuant to section 7, a person is obliged to reimburse litigation expenses together with a party, he and the party are liable for the expenses jointly and severally.

**Section 10**

When party substitution occurs on the plaintiff's side pursuant to chapter 13, section 7, the original plaintiff and his successor are jointly and severally liable for expenses incurred prior to the substitution; after substitution the successor bears sole responsibility.

The successor of an original defendant is solely liable for the litigation expenses.

**Section 11**

When two or more persons are jointly and severally liable for litigation costs, on request of one of them, the court, based upon the particular circumstances, may specify the portion of the expenses that each should ultimately bear, or authorize complete indemnification of one or more by the other.

**Section 12**

As to the liability of an intervenor who lacks party standing to furnish compensation for litigation expenses, and the right of such an intervenor to be compensated for his expenses, the provisions in this chapter concerning parties shall correspondingly apply; however, the intervenor shall be solely liable for the special expenses occasioned by his intervention. Nor may the party supported by the intervenor be directed to furnish compensation for such expenses.

**Section 13**

If disbursements for evidence or any other measure are, by order of the court, to be paid out of public funds or be charged to the parties jointly and severally, the provisions of this chapter concerning the liability to provide reimbursement for litigation expenses shall apply. If each party shall bear his own expenses, such disbursements may be apportioned equally between the parties. Expenses out of public funds for bringing a party to court in custody shall always be paid by that party.

As to reimbursement of advances paid out of public funds on behalf of a person who has been granted legal aid, special provisions have been enacted. (SFS 1972:430)

**Section 14**

A party desiring to be reimbursed for litigation expenses shall make a demand for and present a list of his expenses to the court before the termination of the proceedings. If he fails to do so, he forfeits the right to be reimbursed for expenses incurred in that court, however, despite the absence of a demand, the winning party is entitled to interest as stated in section 8, second paragraph, and to a copy of the judgment or final order of the court at his adversary's expense.

When finally disposing of an action, the court shall simultaneously rule upon the litigation costs and upon the issues mentioned in section

13, first paragraph. If counsel fees are to be reimbursed, the amount of the fees shall be separately stated. (SFS 1982:1123)

**Section 15**

The determination concerning liability to provide compensation for litigation costs incurred in an appellate court in an appeal from a court below shall be based upon the outcome of the action in that court.

As to liability for expenses incurred in a higher court when the proceeding concerns an issue separately appealed to that court, the provisions in this chapter as to actions instituted in lower courts shall correspondingly apply.

If an action is referred back to a court below, the issue of expenses incurred in the higher court shall be determined by the court below when it rehears the case.

# II Proceedings in Criminal Cases

## Chapter 19

### Rules of Competence

**Section 1**

The court for the place in which an offence was committed has competence to try the offence. The offence shall be considered committed at the place in which the criminal act was done and, if the offence was completed or, if an attempt, would have been completed at another place, also at that place. If the offence was committed at places in different court districts it may be tried by any of the courts. If the offence was committed on a Swedish vessel or aircraft during a journey in or outside the realm, competence to try the offence also resides in the court for the place at which the suspect first arrived on board the vessel or aircraft, or in which he was apprehended or otherwise sojourns.

If the place where the offence was committed has not been ascertained when a prosecution is instituted, the case may be entertained by the court for any of the places in which the offence may reasonably be thought to have been committed, or for the place in which the suspect was apprehended or otherwise sojourns.

The prosecution of an offence may also be entertained by the court in which the suspect is required to defend in civil actions in general, or by the court for the place in which he regularly maintains himself, provided that the court, in view of the inquiry, costs, and other circumstances, finds it appropriate. (SFS 1957:299)

**Section 2**

Unless as to a particular case the Government prescribes otherwise, the prosecution of an offence committed at a place outside the realm, or on a foreign vessel or aircraft during a journey in or outside the realm, shall be entertained by the court in which the suspect is required to defend in civil actions in general or by the court at the place in which he was apprehended or otherwise sojours. (SFS 1974:573)

**Section 3**

Prosecutions against two or more persons for joint commission of an offence, when commenced simultaneously, may be instituted in the court at which any of them is required to defend. When the prosecutions are initiated at different times, the court entertaining a prosecution against any one of the alleged offenders may also entertain the prosecution against any other.

The aforesaid shall also apply to prosecutions against two or more persons for offences connected with each other, provided that the court, in view of the inquiry, costs, and other circumstances, finds it appropriate to entertain prosecutions at the same court. (SFS 1948:453)

**Section 4**

A liability claim for false or unjustified prosecution, false accusation, or other untrue statement resulting in a prosecution, may be instituted at the court in which the offence was prosecuted. (SFS 1948:453)

**Section 5**

A procedural offence shall be adjudicated by the court entertaining the proceedings during which the offence occurred.

When a person commits an offence of another kind before a court in session, the same court may adjudicate the offence if adjudication by that court is found appropriate in view of the nature of the offence and other circumstances.

**Section 6**

When a person has committed two or more offences, all of the offences may be tried by a court competent to entertain the prosecution of any of them, provided that the court, in view of the inquiry, costs, and other circumstances, finds it appropriate.

**Section 7**

After the summons has been served upon the suspect, any alteration of the facts determining the court's competence shall be of no legal effect.

If a public prosecution is entertained by a specified court, and another court is also competent, the former court, for extraordinary cause, on request of the prosecutor, may transfer the prosecution to the latter court. All orders and other measures of the former court shall remain effective until the court to which the action is transferred directs otherwise. (SFS 1954:432)

**Section 8**

When dismissing an action on the ground that the court is not a proper forum, the court, pending institution of the action in a competent court, may issue any order which cannot be deferred without risks.

**Section 9**

When it is prescribed by law that a prosecution shall be entertained by a higher court as a court of first instance, or by law or decree that the prosecution shall be entertained by a general lower court other than the one in which the suspect, pursuant to section 1 or 2, is required to defend, no prosecution may be entertained by any other court by reason of the provisions in this chapter. When issues of criminal liability shall be entertained by an authority other than a court, or by a special court, the provisions in this chapter shall not govern.

Any agreement in which a person has promised to institute a prosecution, or to defend at a specified court, shall be without effect. (SFS 1965:585)

**Section 10**

When a lower court has entertained an action, the issue of the competence of that court may not be reviewed by a higher court, unless the issue is appealed to the higher court, or is raised there for the first time by a party entitled to do so, or the action must be entertained by an authority other than a court, or by a special court, or by a higher court as a court of first instance, or by a general lower court other than the one in which the suspect, pursuant to section 1 or 2, is required to defend.

**Section 11**

When a higher court renders an order that the court below lacked competence to entertain a case instituted in that court, the higher court, on request of a party, may refer the action to a competent court below.

When more than one court has dismissed an action for lack of competence, and ordinary appellate proceedings are time-barred, the Supreme Court, on the application of a party, if it finds any of the courts competent, may refer the action to the court by which the action should have been entertained.

### Section 12

The provisions in this chapter shall correspondingly apply to issues of the authority of the courts with regard to preliminary investigations and application of coercive measures.

## Chapter 20

### Right (Standing) to Prosecute; Injured Persons

### Section 1

No issue of criminal liability may be entertained by the court unless a prosecution for the offence has been instituted. However, the court may entertain without prosecution the question of liability for a procedural offence.

### Section 2

Unless otherwise prescribed, public prosecutors have standing to prosecute for offences falling within the domain of public prosecution.

As to the standing of exceptional prosecutors to prosecute for offences falling within the domain of public prosecution, specially enacted provisions shall apply.

Prosecutors may appeal to a higher court even for the benefit of the suspect.

### Section 3

All offences not explicitly exempted therefrom fall within the domain of public prosecution.

If a special condition is prescribed for public prosecution, such as permission by an authority, or accusation by an injured person, that provision shall apply.

**Section 4**

If the same act constitutes more than one offence, and any of the offences falls within the domain of public prosecution, public prosecution may take place as to all of them.

If a person has been accused of an offence that falls within the domain of public prosecution only upon accusation by an injured person, and two or more persons are suspected of having joined in the commission of the offence, public prosecution may take place against all of them.

**Section 5**

An injured person may report an offence for prosecution at the office of any prosecutor or police authority. If the accusation has been made to an authority at a place other than one in which the prosecution may be instituted, the accusation shall be transmitted immediately to the authority at a place appropriate for institution of the prosecution.

**Section 6**

Unless otherwise prescribed, prosecutors must institute actions for offences falling within the domain of public prosecution. (SFS 1964:166)

**Section 7**

Prosecutors may decide not to prosecute, (waiver of prosecution) if:

1. it may be presumed that in the event of prosecution a sanction more severe than fine would not be imposed and the public interest does not require prosecution of the suspect; or

2. the offence was committed before the suspect was sentenced for another offence committed by him or had completely fulfilled the sentence or other sanction for that other offence, and it is evident that the instant offence, compared with the other offence, is, with regard to the sanction, without appreciable importance; or

3. special reasons otherwise make it plain that no sanction is required to prevent the suspect from engaging in further criminal activity and that, in view of the circumstances, no other consideration warrants institution of a prosecution; or

4. it is clear that the offence was committed under the influence of the kind of mental abnormality described in chapter 33, section 2, of the Penal Code, that confinement for psychiatric treatment or treatment in a nursing home or special hospital for the mentally retarded will occur without proceedings, and that no special considerations require prosecution.

Decisions under 3 above may be rendered only by the Chief State Prosecutor.

Any decision not to prosecute for an offence may be withdrawn if sufficient cause for the decision ceases to exist. (SFS 1981:1285)

**Section 7 a**

A decision to waive prosecution may be rendered also after institution of prosecution if such circumstances emerge as, if they had existed or been known at the time of the prosecution, would have led to waiver of prosecution. Prosecution may not be waived, however, if the defendant is opposed thereto or if judgment has already been rendered. (SFS 1981:1285)

**Section 8**

The injured person may not institute a prosecution for an offence falling within the domain of public prosecution unless he has made an accusation to a competent authority and the prosecutor has decided that no prosecution shall take place.

When a prosecutor has instituted a prosecution, the injured person may support the prosecution; he may also appeal to a higher court.

The provision in the first paragraph does not apply to the right of an injured person to institute a prosecution for false or unjustified prosecution, false accusation, or any other untrue statement concerning an offence.

The injured person is the one against whom the offence was committed, or who was affronted or harmed by it. (SFS 1964:166)

**Section 9**

After the entry of judgment, no public prosecution may be withdrawn.

When a public prosecution is withdrawn on the ground that there is insufficient cause to believe that the suspect is guilty of the offence, the injured person may take over the prosecution; he must, however, notify the court of his intention to continue the prosecution. This notice must be given within the period fixed by the court commencing from the time when the injured party was apprised of the prosecutor's withdrawal. The period may not exceed one month. If the injured party does not take over the prosecution, he may not thereafter institute a prosecution for the offence; if requested by the suspect, a judgment of acquittal shall be entered.

**Section 10**

The provisions in sections 8 and 9 concerning the right of the injured person to institute a prosecution or to take over an instituted prosecution do not apply to offences committed in the exercise of his office or commission by:

1. a cabinet minister,

2. Justice of the Supreme Court or Justice of the Supreme Administrative Court,

3. a Parliamentary Ombudsman or anyone who has officiated in his stead,

4. any other officer whom, according to the Parliament Act or other statute, only one of the standing committees or other parliamentary body is competent to prosecute for such an offence, or

5. the Attorney General or anyone who has officiated in his stead. (SFS 1981:1312)

**Section 11**

When with respect to the same offence there are two or more injured persons, any accusation made or prosecution instituted by one of them shall enure to the benefit of all.

**Section 12**

When the injured person, by settlement out of court or otherwise, has promised not to accuse or institute a prosecution against the alleged offender, or when he has withdrawn his accusation or prosecution, he may thereafter neither accuse nor prosecute the offender. If the offence falls within the domain of public prosecution only upon accusation by an injured party, and the promise was made or the accusation withdrawn before the institution of a public prosecution, no such prosecution may take place thereafter.

**Section 13**

When a criminal act has resulted in the death of a person, the decedent's surviving spouse, direct heir, father, mother, brother or sister has the same standing as an injured person to accuse or prosecute the offender.

When the person against whom the offence was committed, or who was affronted or harmed by it, otherwise dies, the persons closely related to him as aforesaid have the same standing to accuse or prosecute the offender as the deceased had, unless the circumstances indicate that the deceased would not have accused or prosecuted the offender. (SFS 1971:875)

### Section 14

If the injured person is a minor and the offence concerns either property over which he does not exercise control or a legal transaction which he is not competent to effect, his legal representative shall have standing to accuse or prosecute the offender. If the offence concerns a personal injury to the minor, the person who has custody of him shall have standing to accuse or prosecute the offender. The provisions in chapter 11, sections 2–5, concerning parties and legal representatives in civil actions shall correspondingly apply to injured persons even if such persons do not themselves prosecute.

As to attorneys for injured persons the provisions in chapter 12 shall apply. (SFS 1974:239)

### Section 15

When the injured person is examined in consequence of the prosecutor's cause, he is entitled to compensation and advance payment pursuant to the provisions concerning witnesses. (SFS 1954:432)

### Section 15 a

An injured party who is heard by reason of the prosecutor's cause and who, in view of the nature of the offence or otherwise, may be assumed to be in need of personal support during the trial may be accompanied by a suitable person to afford such support. (SFS 1984:400)

### Section 16

When prescribed by law or decree that the prosecution of an offence may be instituted by a private person other than the injured person, that private person shall be treated as an injured person with respect to his standing to accuse or participate in the prosecution of the offender, as well as in regard to a prosecution instituted by him.

# Chapter 21

## The Suspect and his Defence

### Section 1

The suspect may himself conduct his defence. If he is a minor, the court, if it is found necessary in view of the nature of the offence or otherwise, shall hear the person who has custody of him; the custodian also has the right to conduct the defence on behalf of the minor.

If the suspect has died, his surviving spouse, direct heir, father, mother, brother or sister may appeal from a judgment to the extent that it declares that the suspect has committed the charged offence. (SFS 1971:875)

**Section 2**

In a public prosecution the suspect is required to attend the main hearing in the lower court in person unless there is no cause to sentence him to a sanction other than fine and his presence can be assumed to be unimportant for the inquiry. In a private prosecution the suspect shall attend the aforesaid hearing in person unless his presence can be assumed to be unimportant for the inquiry. At the main hearing in the court of appeals the suspect shall attend in person if he has been sentenced by the lower court to imprisonment for not less than six months or if there is cause to impose such a sentence upon him, as well as in other situations, unless his presence can be assumed to be unimportant for the inquiry. At the main hearing in the Supreme Court the suspect must appear in person if his presence is found necessary for the inquiry. In the lower court the suspect shall also attend a preparatory hearing in person if the preparation can be assumed to be promoted thereby. At hearings other than those just mentioned the suspect must appear in person if his presence is found necessary.

If the suspect is mentally ill or feeble- minded and the court finds that examination of him would serve no purpose, his attendance in person is not required.

When the suspect is required to appear in person, the court shall notify him to attend.

When the suspect is not required to appear in person, his defence may be presented by attorney. As to attorneys, the provisions in chapter 12 shall apply. (SFS 1981:214)

**Section 3**

In preparing and conducting his defence the suspect may be assisted by defence counsel.

The defence counsel shall be chosen and designated by the suspect. If the suspect is a minor under eighteen years of age, or mentally ill or feeble-minded, the defence counsel shall be designated by his custodian. If the suspect has appointed an attorney, the attorney shall act as defence counsel.

A person may not be defence counsel if he has or has had a commission on behalf of the suspect or financial relations with him and the circumstances are calculated to diminish the confidence in his ability to observe the duties of defence counsel as stated in section 7, first paragraph. As to defence counsel the provisions of chapter 12, sections 2–5 and section 6, second paragraph, shall apply. (SFS 1983:920)

**Section 3 a**

If the suspect is under arrest or in detention, a public defence counsel shall be appointed for him if he so requests. A public defence counsel shall also be appointed, on request, for a person who is suspected of an offence the statutory sanction for which is not more lenient than imprisonment for six months.

A public defence counsel shall be appointed furthermore

1. if the suspect is in need of defence counsel having regard to the investigation of the offence,

2. if defence counsel is needed in view of the fact that it is doubtful what sanction should be chosen and there is reason to impose a sanction other than a fine or a conditional sentence or such sentences in combination, or

3. if special reasons exist in other respect's having regard to the suspect's personal circumstances or the matter att issue.

If the suspect is assisted by a defence counsel designated by him, no public defence counsel shall be appointed in addition to the latter. (SFS 1983:920)

**Section 4**

Public defence counsel is appointed by the court; when the court has disposed of a case, it may, pending an appeal by the suspect, or the expiration of time for an appeal, appoint a defence counsel to assist the suspect in the higher court.

The issue of appointing a public defence counsel shall be considered when an application therefor is made, or when the court otherwise finds cause for consideration of the question.

**Section 5**

Public defence counsel shall be drawn from the corps of advocates found suitable for such assignment. For special cause a person may serve as defence counsel who has passed the test of knowledge prescribed for qualification to judgeship. Principally the court should engage advocates who regularly function as attorneys at the court.

If the suspect has proposed as his public defence counsel someone competent to serve as such, the person proposed shall be appointed unless his employment would occasion considerably increased costs or special reasons otherwise indicate that the appointment should not be made. (SFS 1972:430)

### Section 6

The appointment of a public defence counsel may be revoked by the court if the need for public defence counsel ceases or any other just cause therefor exists. When the suspect himself designates another defence counsel, the appointment shall be revoked unless extraordinary inconvenience would be caused thereby.

A public defence counsel may not delegate his responsibilities to another without consent of the court.(SFS 1983:920)

### Section 7

Defence counsel shall protect the rights of the suspect with zeal and care and, to this end, shall strive to elucidate the cause properly.

Defence counsel should prepare the defence as soon as possible through conference with the suspect.

### Section 8

During the preliminary investigation and the processing of the action at the court, defence counsel may make any request, or take any measure, required to protect the rights of the suspect and, if the case is appealed, defence counsel may assist the suspect in the higher court.

### Section 9

Defence counsel for an arrested or detained person may not be denied access to him. Defence counsel may speak in private with the arrested or detained person; however, a counsel other than a public defence counsel may do so only upon consent of the investigation authority or the prosecutor, or when the court finds a private conference may occur without detriment to the investigation or to order or security at the place of detention.

Public defence counsel, as well as a defence counsel commissioned by the suspect whose commission has been reported to the court, shall be called to attend the main hearing and other court sessions.

### Section 10

Public defence counsel is entitled to reasonable compensation out of public funds for effort, expenditure of time and costs incurred in performing his commission. In determining what is a reasonable fee, consideration shall be paid to the nature and extent of the commission, as also to other circumstances of significance, such as the skill and the trouble devoted to the task and the time spent on it. If the defence counsel has advised the suspect in the matter under the Legal Aid Act (1972:429), a deduction shall be made for the advisory fee received by the defence counsel.

The Government or an authority determined by the Government decides the tariff to be adopted in determining the compensation.

Public defence counsel may not demand further compensation from the suspect. If a private arrangement to this end has been made, it shall be without effect. (SFS 1983:920)

### Section 11

A custodian heard pursuant to section 1 is entitled to compensation and advance payment as provided for a witness. The compensation shall be paid out of public funds. (SFS 1971:240)

## Chapter 22

### Private Claims in Consequence of Crime

### Section 1

A private claim against the suspect or a third person in consequence of an offence may be consolidated with the prosecution of the offence. When the private claim is not entertained in conjunction with the prosecution, the claim shall be instituted in the manner prescribed for civil actions.

### Section 2

When a private claim is based upon an offence falling within the domain of public prosecution, the prosecutor, on request of the injured person, has the duty to prepare and present together with the prosecution the injured person's claim provided that it can be done without inconvenience and that the civil claim is not found devoid of merit. If the injured person wishes to have his claim instituted together with the prosecution, he shall notify the investigation authority or the prosecutor of the claim and state the circumstances upon which it is based.

During the investigation of an offence, if the investigation authority or the prosecutor finds that a private claim may be based on the offence, he shall, if possible, notify the injured person in sufficient time prior to institution of the prosecution.

The first and second paragraphs are correspondingly applicable when the claim has been taken over by another. (SFS 1969:588)

### Section 3

When a private claim in consequence of an offence is independently pending in the court, the court, if it is found appropriate, may direct that the claim be consolidated with the prosecution.

### Section 4

As to the right of the suspect or anyone against whom the injured person asserts a claim, or of a third person, to institute for joint processing with the prosecution a claim of the kind described in chapter 14, section 5, the provisions in that section shall correspondingly apply.

### Section 5

When a private claim has been consolidated with the prosecution, the court, for cause, may direct that the claim be disposed of separately in the manner prescribed for civil actions.

### Section 6

When a prosecution is withdrawn or dismissed without reaching the merits, or when the injured person is declared to have forfeited his right to prosecute the offender, the court, on request of a party, shall direct that the private claim be disposed of as a separate action in the manner prescribed for civil actions. If such a request is not made, the claim shall be dismissed without prejudice.

If a party withdraws his private claim after the adverse party has responded to the merits, the claim shall nonetheless be tried on the merits if the adverse party so requests.

If such a request is not made, the claim shall be dismissed without prejudice.

### Section 7

If a private claim based upon an offence is consolidated with the prosecution and it is found that the act charged is not criminal, the private claim may nonetheless be adjudicated on the merits in the proceeding. (SFS 1969:588)

### Section 8

A private claim based on an offence subject to general prosecution as referred to in chapter 20, section 10 may not be instituted by the injured person unless public prosecution is commenced or the claim is supported by a person who is competent to initiate such prosecution. (SFS 1981:1312)

## Chapter 23

### Preliminary Investigation

#### Section 1

A preliminary investigation shall be initiated as soon as, based upon an accusation or otherwise, there is cause to believe that an offence falling within the domain of public prosecution has been committed. This applies except as otherwise provided in section 4 a or 22.

If an accusation is required for the offence to fall within the domain of public prosecution, a preliminary investigation may be initiated nevertheless without accusation if there is a risk in awaiting accusation. In such case the injured party shall be notified as soon as possible. If he does not then furnish the accusation required for prosecution, the preliminary investigation shall be discontinued. (SFS 1982:184)

#### Section 2

During the preliminary investigation, inquiry shall be made concerning the person who reasonably may be suspected of the offence and concerning the existence of sufficient cause for his prosecution, and the case shall be prepared so that the evidence can be brought forward at the main hearing in an uninterrupted sequence.

#### Section 3

The preliminary investigation is initiated either by a police authority or by the prosecutor. If it is initiated by a police authority and the matter is not of a simple nature, the prosecutor shall take over its conduct as soon as someone can reasonably be suspected of the offence. For special cause the prosecutor shall also take over the direction of the investigation in other situations.

When the investigation is conducted by a police authority, the prosecutor may issue instructions concerning its development.

When the investigation is conducted by the prosecutor, in the course of it he may invoke the assistance of a police authority or commission a policeman to take a special measure relating to the investigation if the nature of the measure so permits.

Before the initiation of a preliminary investigation a policeman may interrogate and take other measure to investigate the offence if the measure cannot be postponed without inconvenience. (SFS 1969:588)

### Section 4

At the preliminary investigation not only circumstances pointing to the guilt of the suspect, but also those favourable to him shall be considered, and any item of evidence beneficial to him shall be preserved. The investigation should be conducted so that no person is unnecessarily exposed to suspicion or put to unnecessary expense or inconvenience.

The preliminary investigation shall be conducted as speedily as the circumstances permit. When there is no longer any cause for pursuing the investigation, it shall be discontinued.

### Section 4 a

A preliminary investigation may also be discontinued

1. if continued investigation would incur costs not in reasonable proportion to the importance of the matter and it can also be assumed that, in the event of prosecution, the offence would not lead to a serverer penalty than a fine, or

2. if it can be assumed that prosecution of the offence would not occur owing to provisions governing waiving of prosecution in chapter 20 or if a special examination of the grounds for prosecution and preliminary investigation are not required in the public interest.

If the conditions for discontinuing a preliminary investigation as stated in the first paragraph exist before such investigation has been initiated, it may be decided that a preliminary investigation shall not be initiated.

An order pursuant to this Article is issued by a prosecutor. An order may be issued solely by the Chief Public Prosecutor when it can be assumed that prosecution would be waived pursuant to chapter 20, section 7, first paragraph (3). (SFS 1982:184)

### Section 5

If pursuant to chapter 21, section 3 a, a public defence counsel shall be assigned to the suspect, the investigation authority shall notify the court thereof. (SFS 1983:920)

### Section 6

During the preliminary investigation, any person may be examined who can be thought to possess information of importance for the investigation.

## Section 7

If a person who has been directed to appear for examination fails to obey the directive without valid excuse, and the distance between the place fixed for the examination and that in which he is resident or where he sojourned at the time of receipt of the notice to attend is not more than fifty kilometres, he may be taken in custody and brought to the examination.

Without any previous notice to attend, any person sojourning within a distance of fifty kilometres from the place in which the examination shall be held may be taken in custody and brought to the examination if the investigation concerns an offence punishable by imprisonment and it may reasonably be expected that he would not obey a notice to attend or, as a result of receiving a notice to attend, would impede the investigation by removal of evidence or in any other way.

When the person to be examined is under arrest or in detention, he shall be brought to the place fixed for the examination. (SFS 1969:588)

## Section 8

By order of a policeman, anyone found at the scene of an offence is obliged to go with the policeman for an examination held immediately after commission of the offence. If he refuses to do so voluntarily without a valid excuse, he may be brought to the examination by the policeman.

## Section 9

A person not under arrest or in detention shall not be obliged to stay for examination more than six hours. If it is of extraordinary importance that a person under suspicion for an offence remain available for continued examination, he shall be obliged to stay an additional six hours.

A person below fifteen years of age shall not be obliged to stay for examination more than three hours. If it is of extraordinary importance for the investigation, the said person shall be obliged to stay an additional three hours.

After termination of the examination, or after the expiration of the time the examined person is obliged to stay, he may immediately leave. Without extraordinary cause he may not be required to appear at a new examination sooner than twelve hours thereafter. (SFS 1984:955)

## Section 10

To the extent possible, a reliable witness commissioned by the investigation authority shall be present at examinations.

The investigating authority has discretion to determine whether any person other than the witness may attend an examination. Upon request of the suspect, he and his defence counsel may be present at an examination held pursuant to section 18, second paragraph. Further, defence counsel may attend any other examination if this can occur without detriment to the investigation.

When the examined person is a minor under fifteen yearsof age, the person having custody of him should be present at the examination if this can occur without detriment to the investigation.

The investigating authority may direct that matters revealed at an examination may not be disclosed.

**Section 11**

When the suspect or his defence counsel is present at an examination, he may, in the order prescribed by the investigating authority, put questions to the examined person. Without permission of the investigating authority, no other person present at an investigation may speak to the examined person during the course of the examination.

**Section 12**

During examination, knowingly incorrect information, promises or hints of special advantage, threats, force, questioning for an unreasonable length of time, or other improper measures may not be used in order to cause a confession or an incriminating statement. The examined person may not be deprived of customary meals or prevented from enjoying required rest.

**Section 13**

If a person refuses to testify concerning a circumstance of importance to the investigation, and he would be obliged to give testimony as a witness in the event of a prosecution, or if it otherwise appears of extraordinary importance for the investigation that a person who would be obliged to testify as a witness at a prosecution be examined as witness while the preliminary investigation is still in progress, then, on the request of the investigating authority, he may be examined as witness before the court.

An examination referred to in the first paragraph may not take place until the preliminary investigation has proceeded so far that a person may reasonably be suspected of the offence. As to the examination, the provisions on proof-taking outside main hearing shall apply to the extent appropriate; the suspect shall be given the opportunity to be present at the examination. Compensation for his appearance shall be paid out of public funds in accordance with the provisions for a defendant who enjoys legal aid. (SFS 1972:430)

**Section 14**

The investigating authority may obtain the opinions of experts. If, in the course of the preliminary investigation, it appears that an expert should at that stage be assigned by the court, the investigating authority may so request. He may also request that the court issue a directive for the production of documentary evidence, or for inspection of an object, or for submission of a public document which may be presumed to be of significance as evidence at the preliminary investigation. (SFS 1980:101)

**Section 15**

If there is a risk that evidence which is to be introduced at the main hearing may be lost prior thereto or be difficult to present at that time, the court, on the request of the investigating authority or the suspect, may immediately take and perpetuate the evidence. To the extent appropriate the provisions on proof-taking outside main hearing shall apply to such proof perpetuation. The expenses for the taking of evidence and for the suspect's appearance at the court shall be paid out of public funds. Compensation for the suspect's appearance shall be paid in accordance with the provisions for a defendant who enjoys legal aid. (SFS 1972:430)

**Section 16**

As to the use of coercive measures during the preliminary investigation, the provisions in chapter 24 to 28 shall apply.

**Section 17**

During the preliminary investigation, if an examination or any other measure is required outside the district of the investigating authority, he may invoke the assistance of the police authority at the place in which the measure shall be taken.

**Section 18**

When the preliminary investigation has proceeded to the point at which a person reasonably is suspected of the offence, that person, when examined, shall be informed of the suspicion. Insofar as is possible without detriment to the investigation, he hand his defence counsel shall be successively furnished an opportunity to be informed of what has taken place at the investigation. They are furthermore entitled to specify the inquiry they consider desirable and to state anything else they regard as required. Notification to this effect shall be given or despatched to the suspect and his defence counsel and they shall be allowed reasonable time for consideration. Prosecution may not be directed until this has been done.

If the suspect requests that a person be examined or that any other inquiry be made, his request shall be complied with if it can be assumed that the measure would be of importance to the investigation. If the request is denied, the reasons therefor shall be stated. (SFS 1981:1294)

**Section 19**

If the investigating authority, although he has concluded the investigation he considers required, has denied a request pursuant to section 18, second paragraph, or if the suspect thinks that there is another defect in the investigation, the suspect may notify the court thereof.

When the notice is filed with the court, it shall consider and rule upon the matter as soon as possible. For cause the court may examine the suspect or any other person, or take any other measure it finds appropriate. Compensation for the suspect's appearance shall be paid in accordance with the provisions for a defendant who enjoys legal aid. (SFS 1972:430)

**Section 20**

Upon the conclusion of the preliminary investigation, a decision shall issue whether or not to institute a prosecution. (SFS 1957:38)

**Section 21**

At the preliminary investigation a protocol shall be kept of matters of importance for the inquiry.

After the testimony of the suspect or any other person is noted, and before the conclusion of the examination, the testimony shall be read out, or an opportunity provided to check the account in another way, and the examined person shall be asked whether he has any objection to the account. Any objection not resulting in correction shall be recorded. Thereafter, the account may not be amended. If an account of testimony is not transcribed into the protocol until after the notes of the account have been checked, the notes shall be attached to the file.

In lesser cases, instead of a protocol, concise notes may be kept of the essentials of the investigation.

As soon as prosecution has been decided upon, the suspect or his defence counsel, on request, shall receive a copy of the protocol or notes of the preliminary investigation. If public defence counsel has been appointed for the suspect, a copy shall be delivered or sent to him without special request. (SFS 1981:1294)

#### Section 22

If there is sufficient cause for prosecution, preliminary investigation pursuant to this chapter is not required concerning offences punishable by fine only or concerning offences referred to in chapter 45, section 2, first or second paragraph. Nor is a preliminary investigation required with respect to offences referred to in chapter 3, section 3, and chapter 7, section 4, second paragraph, unless there is cause for imposition of a sanction other than fine.

If the prosecutor desires to extend the prosecution, that may be done without a preliminary investigation pursuant to this chapter. (SFS 1975:670)

#### Section 23

If additional investigation is found required after the institution of a prosecution, the provisions in this chapter shall apply to it to the extent appropriate.

#### Section 24

Further regulations as to the duties of investigating authorities, concerning notification as stated in section 18, first paragraph, third sentence, and concerning protocols and notes of preliminary investigations are issued by the Government. (SFS 1974:573)

## Chapter 24

### Arrest and Detention

#### Section 1

Anyone suspected on probable cause of an offence punishable by imprisonment for a term of one year or more may be detained if, in view of the nature of the offence, the behaviour of the suspect or any other circumstance, it may reasonably be expected that he will flee or otherwise evade legal proceedings or punishment, or impede the investigation by removal of evidence or by any other device, or if there is cause to believe that he will continue his criminal activity.

If the offence is less grave than stated in the first paragraph but is punishable by imprisonment, and the suspect has no permanent residence within the realm, he may be detained if it may reasonably be expected that he will flee.

If the offence is punishable by imprisonment for a term of at least two years, detention shall occur unless it is evident that there is no cause for it.

If it may be assumed that the suspect will be sentenced only to fine, detention may not occur. (SFS 1975:670)

**Section 2**

Anyone suspected on probable cause of an offence, irrespective of the nature of the offence, may be detained if he is unknown and either avoids giving his name and residence, or there is cause to believe that his statement thereon is untrue, as well as if he lacks a residence within the realm, and it reasonably can be expected that he will seek to avoid legal proceedings or punishment by leaving the realm.

**Section 3**

If, owing to the age of the suspect, his state of health or other similar circumstance, it may be apprehended that detention would be seriously detrimental to him, he may be detained only if it is manifest that adequate supervision cannot be arranged. The same applies to a woman who has given birth so recently that detention may be expected to be seriously detrimental to the child. If the suspect does not wish to submit to supervision, detention shall take place.

Special provisions have been enacted with respect to further restrictions on detention of minors under eighteen years of age.

Chapter 25 prescribes that travel prohibition or obligation to report may be imposed instead of detention. (SFS 1981:1294)

**Section 4**

Detention orders are issued by the court.

**Section 5**

If there is cause for the detention of a person, he may be arrested while awaiting the court's order thereon.

Even if full cause for detention does not exist, the suspect may be arrested if it is found to be of extraordinary importance that he remains in custody pending further investigation.

Arrest orders are issued by the public prosecutor. The order shall contain particulars of the offence to which the suspicion relates and of the grounds for the arrest. (SFS 1981:1294)

**Section 6**

When the person whose arrest has been ordered has fled, or is otherwise not present when the order is issued, notice of the execution of the order shall be reported to the prosecutor as soon as it has occurred.

If a person suspected of an offence flees, and there is cause for his arrest, he may be posted as wanted by the prosecutor. (SFS 1981:1294)

**Section 7**

When there is cause for the arrest of a person, but an order therefor cannot be awaited without risks, any policeman, even without such an order, may apprehend the person.

Anyone may apprehend a person who has committed an offence punishable by imprisonment if he is caught in the very act or running away from the place. Anyone may also apprehend a person wanted for an offence. The apprehended person shall promptly be turned over to the first policeman encountered.

When a person has been apprehended, a report thereof shall promptly be made to the prosecutor; after an examination referred to in section 8, the latter must decide immediately whether the apprehended person shall be arrested or put at liberty. (SFS 1981:1294)

**Section 8**

Anyone arrested pursuant to section 6, or apprehended pursuant to section 7, shall be brought before the prosecutor for examination as soon as possible, or before a policeman commissioned to hold the examination. (SFS 1981:1294)

**Section 9**

When a person is arrested or when an arrest order as stated in section 6 is executed, the arrested person shall be informed of the offence for which he is suspected and the grounds for the arrest. The immediate relatives and anyone in especially close relationship with the arrested person shall be notified of the arrest as soon as this can be done without detriment to the investigation. In the absence of extraordinary cause, however, such notice may not be given against the wish of the arrested person. (SFS 1981:1294)

**Section 10**

When there is no longer any cause for arrest, the suspect shall immediately be put at liberty.

**Section 11**

An arrested person shall be kept in custody, but no further restriction may be placed on his liberty except as required by the purpose of the arrest, discipline at the place of custody, or security of life and property. His retention in custody, or removal from one place to another, shall be effected in a manner that does not attract unnecessary attention.

**Section 12**

Unless the arrested person is put at liberty, the prosecutor shall submit to the court an application for a detention order no later than the day after the issuance of the arrest order, or after the appearance of the arrested person for examination pursuant to section 8. If disposition of the detention issue requires additional investigation, the application may be postponed; however, it shall be submitted as soon as possible, and at latest on the fifth day after the issuance of the arrest order, or after the appearance of the arrested person for examination. When no application as stated in this paragraph is made, the arrested person shall immediately be put at liberty.

The protocol or notes of the preliminary investigation up to the time of the application shall be submitted to the court and to the arrested person and his defence counsel, insofar as they are of importance for consideration of the detention issue, together with the application; with the consent of the court, however, the submission may be deferred for a specified short period of time. When examination of a person other than the arrested one is sought in conjunction with the detention application, a notice thereof shall also be given to the court. (SFS 1981:1294)

**Section 13**

When an application pursuant to section 12 has been filed, the court shall hold a hearing on the detention issue as soon as possible and, if no extraordinary impediment exists, no later than four days after receipt of the application. If the main hearing is scheduled to occur within one week of the filing of the application, the matter may be postponed until the main hearing, unless the court finds that a special hearing should be held.

**Section 14**

At the hearing on the detention issue, the person requesting the detension order shall be present as well as the arrested person unless there is an extraordinary impediment to the latter's appearance.

The person requesting the detention order shall state the circumstances upon which the request is founded. The arrested person and his defence counsel shall be given an opportunity to speak. In the absence of special cause, the inquiry may not extend beyond the contents of the documents from the preliminary investigation and the further statements of the parties. (SFS 1981:1294)

### Section 15

To the extent possible, the hearing shall continue without any recess until the issue can be determined. No postponement may occur in the absence of extraordinary cause; without the consent of the suspect, a postponement may not exceed four days.

When the detention hearing is postponed, the arrest shall continue in effect unless the court orders otherwise.

### Section 16

After the conclusion of the hearing, the court shall immediately pronounce its determination on the detention issue. A detention order shall detail the offence for which the detained person is suspected and briefly state the cause for the detention.

When detention is not ordered, the court shall direct the arrested person to be put immediately at liberty.

### Section 17

The issue of the detention of a person who is not arrested may be considered on request of the prosecutor. After the institution of the prosecution, the court may consider the issue on request of the injured person, as well as on its own motion.

When an issue of detention has been raised, a hearing shall be held by the court as soon as possible. As to such a hearing the provisions in sections 14 to 16, to the extent appropriate, shall apply. If the suspect has been notified to attend the hearing, or there is cause to believe that he has fled or is otherwise avoiding detection, his failure to appear shall not deter the court from holding the hearing. If the injured person fails to appear at the hearing, although he has been notified to attend, the issue may be determined without regard to his absence.

When the court has issued an order for the detention of a person who has not appeared before it, notice of the execution of the order shall be given the court as soon as it has occurred. (SFS 1981:1294)

### Section 18

When the court issues an order pursuant to section 16 for the detention of an arrested person, or pursuant to section 17 for the detention of a person present at the court, or when a notice of the execution of a detention order is filed, the court shall, unless the prosecution is already instituted, fix the time within which the prosecution shall be instituted. The time fixed may not be longer than is found unavoidably necessary.

When the period fixed exceeds two weeks, as long as the suspect is detained and until the prosecution is instituted, the court shall hold a new hearing of the kind specified in sections 14 to 16 at intervals of not more than two weeks and at such hearings inquire particularly to make certain that the investigation is being pursued as speedily as possible. When, in view of the nature of the investigation or any other circumstance, however, it is found evident that a hearing within the time just indicated would be without significance, the court may fix intervals of longer periods.

If the fixed period is found insufficient, upon an application made before the expiration of the period, the court may grant an extension of the time.

**Section 19**

If neither a prosecution has been instituted nor an application for an extension of time filed within the period stated in section 18, or if there is no longer cause for detension, the court shall immediately order that the detained person be put at liberty.

**Section 20**

When an issue of detention is raised in an action appealed to a higher court, that court may determine the issue without a hearing; if the suspect is under arrest, the determination shall be made no later than four days after the application for detention has been submitted to the court. If a hearing is found necessary, it shall be held as soon as possible. As to such a hearing the provisions in sections 14 to 17 shall apply.

**Section 21**

If the suspect is in detention when he is sentenced for the offence, the court shall determine in accordance with the provisions in this chapter whether he shall remain in custody pending conclusiveness of its judgment; if the suspect is at liberty, the court may order his detension.

In applying the first paragraph the provisions in this chapter concerning detension of a person who may reasonably be expected to evade punishment shall govern also in the case of a person who may reasonably be expected to evade deportation. The detention order does not apply, however, during a period when the offender is serving a term of imprisonment to which he has been sentenced in the case. (SFS 1980:378)

### Section 22

A detained person shall be brought to a public jail without delay. If a member of the military forces, however, he may be brought to a military jail.

If, for investigation of the offence for which a detension order has issued or for investigation of another offence of which the detained person is suspected, it is found of extraordinary importance that he be held in custody at a place other than that referred to in the preceding paragraph, the court, on request of the prosecutor, may direct that the transfer to jail be deferred until further notice. The court, the prosecutor may also direct that the detained person, after his transfer to jail, be brought to a place outside the jail for examination or any other measure.

As to the custody of detained persons who are undergoing or have undergone psychiatric examination, special provisions have been enacted. (SFS 1981:1294)

### Section 23

Nor may anyone be held in custody by reason of suspicion of an offence except as prescribed in this chapter or otherwise provided by law, even upon consent.

The duty of a person suspected of an offence to remain for examination is prescribed in chapter 23.

### Section 24

Concerning treatment in custody of arrested or detained persons, and concerning compensation to wrongfully detained persons, special providions have been enacted. (SFS 1966:302)

## Chapter 25

### Travel Prohibition

### Section 1

If anyone reasonably is suspected of an offence punishable by imprisonment and, in view of the nature of the offence, the behaviour of the suspect or any other circumstance, it can be reasonably expected that he will flee or otherwise evade legal proceedings or punishment, but there is otherwise no cause for his arrest or detention, if found sufficient, in lieu of arrest or detention, an order may issue prohibiting him from leaving the place of residence assigned to him or he may be ordered to report at fixed hours to a specified police authority. Irrespective of the nature of the offence, travel prohibition or obligation to report may be ordered if it can be reasonably expected that the suspect, by leaving the realm, will evade legal proceedings or punishment.

If cause exists for detention or arrest of a person, but it can be assumed that the object thereof can be attained by travel prohibition or obligation to report, an order to that effect may be issued also in cases other than referred to in the first paragraph. (SFS 1981:1295)

**Section 2**

In conjunction with travel prohibition or obligation to report, directives may be prescribed requiring the suspect to be present at fixed hours at his place of residence or work. Other condition found necessary for his supervision may also be imposed. Travel prohibition, futhermore, may be combined with obligation to report.

As to obligation to report the provisions concerning travel prohibition shall govern in the application of this code in other respects. (SFS 1981:1294)

**Section 3**

Travel prohibition orders are issued by the prosecutor or the court.

An issue of travel prohibition may be considered by the court on request of the prosecutor or when the court is called upon to determine whether the suspect shall be detained or continued in custody. After the institution of prosecution, the court may consider the issue on request of the injured party, as well as on its own motion.

When an issue of travel prohibition is raised at the court, a hearing thereon shall be held as soon as possible. As to such a hearing, the provisions in chapter 24, section 17, to the extent relevant, shall apply. If delay entails risks, the court may immediately issue an order of travel prohibition to remain effective until it otherwise orders. (SFS 1981:1295)

**Section 4**

A travel prohibition order shall describe the offence of which the person is suspected, and state the place in which the suspect shall sojourn, and anything else he is required to observe. The order shall contain a reminder of the sanction for violation of the prohibition or failure to comply with any condition attached to it.

The order shall be served upon the suspect.

### Section 5

When a travel prohibition has been issued by the prosecutor the suspect may request the court's consideration of the prohibition. On receipt of the request, the court shall hold a hearing of the kind referred to in section 3 as soon as possible and, unless an extraordinary impediment exists, no later than four days after receipt of the request. If the main hearing is scheduled to occur within one week of the filing of the request, however, the hearing may be postponed until the main hearing, unless the court finds that a special hearing should be held. (SFS 1981:1294)

### Section 6

When the court issues a travel prohibition order or confirms such an order, unless the prosecution has already been instituted, it shall fix the time within which the prosecution shall be instituted. The time may not be longer than is found unavoidably necessary. If the travel prohibition order was neither issued nor confirmed by the court, the prosecution shall be instituted within one month of the issuance of the order.

If the period stated in the first paragraph is found insufficient, upon an application made before the expiration of the period, the court may grant an extension thereof.

### Section 7

If neither a prosecution has been instituted, nor an application for extension of time has been filed within the time stated in section 6, or if otherwise there is no longer any cause for travel prohibition, the prohibition shall immediately be terminated.

Termination of travel prohibition shall be ordered by the prosecutor. If the prohibition has been issued or confirmed by the court, the latter shall order its termination. The court may empower the prosecutor to decide on temporary exceptions from the travel prohibition or from directives issued in conjunction therewith.

The provisions in chapter 24, section 21, as to detention shall correspondingly apply to travel prohibition. (SFS 1981:1294)

### Section 8

When an issue of travel prohibition is raised in an action appealed to a higher court, the higher court may determine the issue without a hearing. If a hearing is found necessary, it shall be held as soon as possible. As to such a hearing the provisions in chapter 24, section 17, to the extent relevant, shall apply.

### Section 9

For violation of a travel prohibition, or for failure to comply with a condition attached to it, the suspect shall immediately be arrested or put in detention, unless it is evident that there are no grounds therefor.

## Chapter 26

### Provisional Attachment

### Section 1

If anyone is reasonably suspected of an offence and it can reasonably be expected that, by fleeing, removal of property or otherwise, he will evade the obligation which it can be assumed will be placed upon him by reason of the offence to pay a fine, the value of forfeited property, or any other compensation to the Crown, or damages or any other compensation to an injured party, so much of his property may be placed under provisional attachment as can be assumed to cover the claim in the event of distraint. (SFS 1981:828)

### Section 2

Orders of provisional attachment are issued by the court.

An issue of provisional attachment may be considered on the request of the investigation authority, the prosecutor or the injured party. After the institution of the prosecution the court may also consider such an issue on its own motion.

The investigation authority or prosecutor may request provisional attachment by reason of the existence of an injured person's claim for damages or any other compensation only if the claim has been reported to him by the injured person. The court may order such a measure only upon request.

When an issue of provisional attachment is raised, a hearing thereon shall be held by the court as soon as possible. As to such a hearing the provisions in chapter 24, section 17, to the extent relevant, shall apply. If delay entails risks, the court may immediately direct that the measure remain effective until it otherwise orders. (SFS 1981:828)

### Section 3

While awaiting the court's order of provisional attachment, the investigation authority or the prosecutor may take personal property into custody.

If delay entails risks, such a measure may also be taken by a policeman; however, a report thereof shall promptly be made to the investigating authority or the prosecutor, who must then immediately consider and determine, whether or not the property shall remain in custody. (SFS 1981:828)

**Section 4**

When the investigating authority or the prosecutor has taken personal property into custody, or ordered that such property remain in custody, as soon as possible, and no later than five days thereafter, he shall submit to the court an application for provisional attachment. If no such application is made, the property shall immediately be returned.

On receipt of an application, the court shall hold a hearing of the kind referred to in section 2 as soon as possible and, if no extraordinary impediment exists, no later than four days after receipt of the application. If the main hearing is scheduled to occur within one week of the filing of the application, however, the hearing may be postponed until the main hearing, unless the court finds that a special hearing should be held.

If a provisional attachment is ordered, unless the court prescribes otherwise, the property shall be kept in the custody of the authority that made the application until the order is executed. (SFS 1981:828)

**Section 5**

When the court orders a provisional attachment, unless the prosecution is already instituted, the court shall fix the period within which the prosecution shall be instituted. That period may not be longer than is found unavoidably necessary.

If the fixed period is found insufficient, upon an application made before the expiration of the period, the court may grant an extension thereof. (SFS 1981:828)

**Section 6**

If neither a prosecution has been instituted, nor an application for extension of time has been filed within the time stated in section 5, or if adequate security has been furnished, or if otherwise there is no longer any cause for provisional attachment, the court shall immediately terminate the measure.

When finally adjudicating the action, the court shall determine whether the measure shall continue in effect. In conjunction with its judgment, the court may also order any measure of the kind referred to herein. (SFS 1981:828)

### Section 7

The provisions in chapter 25, section 8, as to travel prohibition shall correspondingly apply to provisional attachment. (SFS 1981:828)

### Section 8

As to execution of provisional attachment the provisions in the Code of Execution shall apply. The court may issue further instructions concerning the execution if required. (SFS 1981:828)

## Chapter 27

### Seizure

### Section 1

Objects which reasonably can be assumed to be of importance for the investigation of an offence, or to have been taken from a person or to be subject to forfeiture by reason of an offence, may be seized.

The provisions in this chapter concerning objects, to the extent nothing to the contrary is prescribed, shall also apply to documents.

### Section 2

No document may be seized if its contents can be assumed to be such that an officer or other person referred to in chapter 36, section 5, may not testify as a witness concerning the document, and the document is possessed by such officer or person, or by the person for whose benefit the obligation to observe secrecy has been imposed. Nor is any written communication between the suspect and anyone related to him as stipulated in chapter 36, section 3, or between persons so related, subject to seizure when in the possession of the suspect or the related person, unless the offence in question is punishable by a minimum of two years imprisonment. (SFS 1964:166)

### Section 3

A letter, telegram or other dispatch which is in the posession of the Post Office or Telecommuncations Administration may be seized only if the offence is punishable by a minimum sentence of imprisonment for one year, and the dispatch would be subject to seizure from the addressee. (SFS 1964:166)

### Section 4

Anyone who lawfully apprehends or arrests a suspect or who effectuates detention or a search of premises or of a person, may seize the objects then revealed.

Objects otherwise found may be seized upon the order of the investigating authority or the prosecutor. If delay entails risks, the measure may be taken by a policeman without such an order, except with respect to dispatches in the possession of the Post Office or Telecommunications Administration.

If a seizure is executed by anyone other than the investigating authority or the prosecutor, and neither of them has ordered the seizure, a report shall promptly be made to him, and he must then immediately consider and determine whether the seizure shall remain in effect.

### Section 5

The court may order seizure of an object presented to the court or otherwise accessible to it.

An issue of seizure may be considered by the court upon request of the investigating authority or the prosecutor. After the institution of the prosecution, the court may consider the issue at the request of the injured party, as well as on its own motion.

When an issue of seizure is raised in the court, a hearing shall be held thereon as soon as possible. As to such a hearing, the provisions in chapter 24, section 17, to the extent relevant, shall apply. If delay entails risks, the court may immediately issue a seizure order to remain effective until otherwise ordered.

### Section 6

When seizure was effected without a court order, the person subjected to the seizure may request court consideration of the issue. On receipt of the request, the court shall hold a hearing of the kind referred to in section 5 as soon as possible and, in the absence of an extraordinary impediment, no later than four days after receipt of the request. If the main hearing is scheduled to occur within one week of the receipt of the request, however, the hearing may be postponed until the main hearing unless the court finds that a special hearing should be held.

### Section 7

When the court issues a seizure order or confirms a seizure already executed, unless prosecution has already been instituted the court shall fix the period within which prosecution shall be instituted. This period may not be longer than is found unavoidably necessary.

In a case other than stated in the first paragraph, prosecution shall be instituted within one month after execution of the seizure unless the value of the seized property is less than one thousand kronor.

If the period stated in the first or second paragraph is found insufficient, the court may grant an extension of the period if an application therefor is filed before the expiration of the period. (SFS 1974:1067)

**Section 8**

If neither a prosecution has been instituted nor an application for extension of time has been filed within the time stated in section 7, or if otherwise there is no longer any cause for the seizure, it shall immediately be terminated.

Termination of a seizure order is directed by the court or, if the court has neither issued nor confirmed the seizure order, by the investigating authority or the prosecutor.

When finally adjudicating the action, the court shall determine whether the seizure shall remain in effect. In conjunction with its judgment the court may also issue a seizure order.

**Section 9**

If there is cause to believe that a dispatch subject to seizure will be received at a postal, telegraph, railway or any other office of conveyance, the court may order that, upon receipt, the dispatch shall be held until the issue of its seizure has been determined. A question of this nature may be considered only upon request of the investigating authority or the prosecutor.

The period during which the order shall be effective must be stated therein; this period may not exceed one month from the time of service of the order upon the office manager. The order shall state that, in the absence of permission of the investigating authority or the prosecutor, neither the sender, the addresee, nor any other person, may be informed of the measure.

When, pursuant to an order of the kind described above, a dispatch has been held, the manager shall notify the authority who requested the measure without delay; that authority must immediately consider and determine whether the dispatch shall be seized.

**Section 10**

Any seized object shall be taken into custody by the executor of the seizure. If it can be done without risk, and is otherwise deemed appropriate, the object may however be left with the possessor. An object left with the possessor shall be sealed or marked as seized unless such measure is evidently unnecessary.

The person from whom an object has been seized may not alienate it nor dispose of it by other means contrary to the purpose of the seizure. An object not taken into custody or sealed may be used by the possessor unless otherwise ordered.

Any seized object shall be carefully preserved, and strict supervision shall be maintained so that the object is neither exchanged, altered, nor put to any other misuse. (SFS 1981:828)

**Section 11**

When the person from whose possession the property is taken is not present at the seizure, he shall be notified of it and of the disposition of the seized property without delay. When a dispatch in the possession of a postal, telegraph, railway or any other office of conveyance is seized, the addressee and also the sender, if he is known, shall be notified of it as soon as this can be done without detriment to the investigation.

**Section 12**

A seized postal or telegraphic communication, account book, or any other private document may not be examined more closely, nor may a letter or any other closed document be opened, except by the court, the investigating authority, or the prosecutor; however, on instruction of the authority just mentioned, the document may be inspected by an expert or any other person employed for, or otherwise examined during, the investigation of the offence. If the executor of the seizure is not authorized to examine the document more closely, it shall be sealed by him.

Any of the aforesaid documents shall be examined as soon as possible. If the addressee can be informed of the contents of a postal or telegraphic communication in its entirety or in part without detriment to the investigation, a copy or an extract of the document shall promptly be delivered to him.

**Section 13**

A record shall be kept of the seizure stating the purpose of the seizure, and the manner in which it was effected, and describing accurately the seized object.

On request, the person subjected to seizure is entitled to receive a certificate of the seizure which shall state the offence under investigation.

**Section 14**

The provisions in chapter 25, section 8, concerning travel prohibition shall correspondingly apply to seizure.

**Section 14 a**

If an object may reasonably be presumed to have been forfeited pursuant to chapter 36, section 3, of the Penal Code, it may be seized. The provisions in this chapter concerning seizure shall apply correspondingly in this respect. (SFS 1975:403)

**Section 15**

For the security of the investigation of an offence, a building or room may be closed off, admission to a specific area enjoined, removal of a specific object prohibited, or any other measure taken.

As to any of the aforesaid measures, the provisions in this chapter concerning seizure, to the extent relevant, shall apply.

**Section 16**

If a person reasonably can be suspected of an offence punishable by imprisonment for at least two years, and it is found of extraordinary importance for the investigation that the investigating authority or the prosecutor obtains knowledge of conversation to and from the suspect's telephone or any other telephone that can be assumed to be used by him, the court may authorize wire-tapping of the conversations. The question of such authorization may be considered by the court only on request of the investigating authority or the prosecutor.

Authority for a wire-tap shall contain a time limitation, not to exceed one week from service of the authorization upon the manager of the telephone office. If, however, the suspicion relates to a grave drug offence or to grave smuggling of drugs pursuant to section 1 of the Ordinance relating to Narcotic Drugs (1962:704), wire-tapping may be authorized for at most one month from the said date.

As to inspection of the records of a wire-tap, the provisions in section 12, first paragraph, on examination and inspection of private documents shall correspondingly apply. To the extent that the record contains matters of no importance for the investigation, it shall be destroyed immediately after inspection. (SFS 1981:214)

**Section 17**

If provisions concerning seizure contained in any law or decree are inconsistent with the regulations contained in this chapter, the former shall govern.

## Chapter 28

### Search of Premises and Search and Examination of Persons

#### Section 1

If there is cause to believe that an offence punishable by imprisonment has been committed, any house, room, or closed place of storage may be searched in order to uncover any object which is subject to seizure, or otherwise to detect any circumstance which may be of importance for the investigation of the offence.

However, a search of the premises of a person other than one who reasonably can be suspected of the offence may be executed only if the offence was committed there, or the suspect was apprehended there, or extraordinary cause otherwise appears indicating that the search will reveal an object subject to seizure or any other information concerning the offence.

Nor may the consent of the suspect be invoked to justify a search of his premises unless he personally initiated the request for the search. (SFS 1964:166)

#### Section 2

For detection of a person who is to be apprehended, arrested or detained, taken in custody for examination or appearance in court, or subjected to bodily search or examination of persons, a search of his premises may be made; the premises of any other person may also be searched if extraordinary cause exists indicating that the person sought is present there. (SFS 1984:388)

#### Section 3

A place accessible to the public or usually frequented by vagrants or criminals, or where objects of the kind sought are usually purchased or pawned, may be searched for the purposes stated in section 1 or 2 even in circumstances other than those dealt with in sections 1 and 2.

#### Section 4

Orders for the search of premises are issued by the investigating authority, the prosecutor, or the court. When the search can be assumed to be on a large scale, or to cause extraordinary inconvenience to the person at whose premises the search is conducted, the search should not be made without a court order unless a delay would entail risks.

An issue concerning search of premises may be considered by the court upon the request of the investigating authority or the prosecutor. After the institution of the prosecution, the court may also consider such an issue on request of the injured party, as well as on its own motion.

### Section 5

A policeman may conduct a search of premises without the search order prescribed in section 4 if the measure has as its purpose detection of a person who is to be apprehended, arrested or detained, or taken in custody for examination or appearance in court, or seizure of an object that has been pursued or traced directly from the scene of an offence; such a search may also be conducted in other situations in which delay entails risks.

### Section 6

At a search of premises, inconvenience or damages may not be caused beyond what is unavoidable.

If it is required, a room or a place of storage may be opened by force. When this has been done, on completion of the examination, the room or place shall be appropriately restored to the condition in which it was found.

In the absence of special cause, premises may not be searched between nine o'clock in the evening and six o'clock in the morning.

### Section 7

Whenever possible, a reliable witness commissioned by the officer undertaking the search shall be present at a search of premises. The officer undertaking the search may obtain required assistance from an expert or any other person.

The person whose premises are searched or, if he is not present, his household servants in attendance, shall be given an opportunity to oversee the search, as well as to call a witness, but without delaying the search thereby. When neither the person whose premises were searched nor any of his servants nor a witness called by them was present, the person whose premises were searched must be notified of the measure taken as soon as this can be done without detriment to the investigation.

During the search the presence of an injured person, or his attorney, may be permitted so that he may furnish necessary information; however, care shall be taken to assure that the injured person or the attorney does not obtain knowledge of the circumstances revealed at the search to a greater extent than necessitated by the reason for his presence.

**Section 8**

A postal or telegraphic communication, an account book or any other private document found at search of premises may not be more closely examined, nor may a letter or any other closed document be opened, in a manner other than prescribed in chapter 27, section 12, paragraph 1.

**Section 9**

A record shall be kept of a search of premises, stating the purpose of the search and what occurred thereat.

On request, anyone whose premises have been searched is entitled to receive a certificate thereof which shall state the offence under investigation.

**Section 10**

For the purposes stated in section 1 or 2, the investigation authority or the prosecutor, as well as a policeman, may search a place other than one mentioned in section 1, even if the place is not accessible to the public.

**Section 11**

If there is cause to believe that an offence punishable by imprisonment has been committed, a personal search may be made in order to look for an object subject to seizure, or otherwise to discover a circumstance that can be of importance for investigation of the offence.

As to a person other than one who reasonably can be suspected of the offence, however, a search may be made only for extraordinary cause indicating that thereby an object subject to seizure will be found or other information concerning the offence will be gained. (SFS 1964:166)

**Section 12**

A bodily search of the person who reasonably can be suspected of an offence punishable by imprisonment may be made for the purposes stated in section 11.

In conducting a personal search, if required, a speciment of blood may be taken and any other examination that can be accomplished without appreciable detriment may be made. (SFS 1964:166)

**Section 13**

As to bodily search and examination the provisions in sections 4, 8 and 9 concerning search of premises shall apply to the extent relevant.

A bodily search or examination of extensive dimension shall be made indoors and in a separate room. If it is made by anyone other than a physician, a reliable witness commissioned by the officer conducting the search shall be present whenever possible. A specimen of blood may not be taken by any person other than a physician or qualified nurse.

A bodily search of a woman may not be made or witnessed by any person other than a woman, a physician or a qualified nurse. The same applies to bodily examination and other examination in conjunction therewith than the taking of blood samples. (SFS 1981:1294)

### Section 14

A person arrested or detained may be photographed or fingerprinted; he may also be subjected to any similar measure. The same shall apply to any other person if such measures are needed in order to obtain information concerning an offence punishable by imprisonment.

Further regulations as to the aforesaid measures are issued by the Government. (SFS 1974:573)

### Section 15

If provisions as to search of premises or bodily search and examination contained in any law or decree are inconsistent with the regulations contained in this chapter, the former shall govern.

## Chapter 29

### Voting

### Section 1

During the deliberation on a judgment or order, if diverging opinions are expressed, voting shall take place.

During voting, opinions shall be declared by the judges in reverse order of their length of service except that, regardless of seniority, the court's chairman votes last. When a judge of the panel has presided at the preparation of the case, he states his opinion first. If lay judges sit in the court, the latter state their opinion last.

Each member of a court shall state the grounds upon which he rests his opinion. (SFS 1983:370)

### Section 2

The court shall vote separately upon procedural issues.

When the defendant is charged with several offences in the same proceeding, the court shall, if necessary, with respect to each offence first vote whether the accused is guilty of the offence, and then upon the sanction. It shall also vote separately on whether one or multiple offences are involved if that question should arise.

With respect to the sanction, if there are divergent opinions whether a sanction other than punishment shall be imposed, or whether such sanction shall be coupled with a fine, or whether probation shall be coupled with institutional treatment pursuant to chapter 28, section 3, of the Penal Code, separate voting, if required, shall take place upon each opinion upon which one of the members demands that a vote be taken. The aforesaid shall also apply to the questions whether all sanctions shall be completely dispensed with and whether the defendant shall be free from all sanctions on the ground that he committed the offence under the influence of mental abnormality. When such an opinion does not prevail, a separate vote on the punishment shall take place.

When there are divergent opinions upon the amount of fine to be coupled with a sanction other than punishment, upon the term of imprisonment to be coupled with probation pursuant to chapter 28, section 3, of the Penal Code, or upon special directives for probation, separate voting upon these issues shall, if necessary, take place.

A member of the court who has been outvoted on a particular issue is obliged to participate in subsequent votings, accepting as a premise thereof the position of the majority on the issue as to which he dissented; however, when voting on imposing a punishment, or on the issue whether all sanctions shall be completely dispensed with, or whether the accused shall be free from all sanctions on the ground that he committed the offence under the influence of mental abnormality, anyone who has previously voted for acquittal of the defendant shall be considered to have supported the opinion most lenient to the defendant. (SFS 1981:214)

### Section 3

In Voting, the opinion of the majority shall prevail. If one of the opinions has obtained half of the votes and that opinion is the most lenient, it shall prevail; when there has been separate voting on whether a conditional sentence shall be given, or probation, or probation coupled with imprisonment pursuant to chapter 28, section 3, of the Penal Code, imposed, or an order of surrender for special care issued, the opinion shall prevail that has obtained half of the votes and, among them, that of the chairman. The same applies in other situations in which no opinion can be considered more lenient than any other. (SFS 1983:370)

### Section 4

If, in a vote referred to in section 3, there are more than two opinions, none of which prevails, the votes most unfavourable to the defendant shall be counted with the votes next most unfavourable and, if necessary, the counting shall continue on the same basis until some opinion prevails; when no opinion can be considered more adverse to the defendant than any other, the opinion obtaining more votes than any other or, if two or more opinions have an equal number of votes, that supported by the most prominent member among those voting for one of these opinions shall prevail. (SFS 1983:370)

### Section 5

If there is a disagreement about how voting shall proceed, or which opinion shall prevail, the disagreement shall be resolved by voting.

### Section 6

As to voting upon procedural issues that do not concern criminal liability, or upon private claims, or upon issues subject to section 5 or concerning the assessment of litigation costs, the provisions in chapter 16 shall govern; however, as to detention or measures stated in chapter 25–28, the provisions in this chapter as to voting on criminal liability shall apply. When a private claim is joined with a criminal prosecution, the court's finding of liability on the criminal charge is binding for the adjudication of the private claim. (SFS 1983:370)

### Section 7

Repealed by SFS 1983:370.

## Chapter 30

### Judgments and Orders

### Section 1

The final determination of an action upon the merits is a judgment. Any other court decision is an order. An order finally severing an action from the court otherwise than by a judgment is a final order. An order rendered by a higher court upon an issue separately appealed to that court also constitutes a final order.

### Section 2

If the court has held a main hearing, the judgment shall be based upon the material presented at that hearing. A judge may not participate in the judgment unless present throughout the main hearing. If a new main hearing has been held, the judgment shall be based upon material presented at that hearing.

When an action is adjudicated without a main hearing, the judgment shall be based upon the contents of the documents and anything else that has occurred in the action.

### Section 3

A judgment may not concern any act other than one for which a claim of criminal liability was properly brought or as to which it has been otherwise prescribed by law that the court may entertain a question of criminal liability. The court shall not be restricted by a party's legal characterization of the offence, nor by a party's specification of the operative statutory provision.

### Section 4

When several prosecutions are joined in a single action, the court may enter a judgment upon any of them separately, although the processing of the remaining ones has not been terminated. If the prosecutions concern the same defendant, however, such a judgment may not be entered in the absence of extraordinary cause. (SFS 1956:587)

### Section 5

A judgment shall be in writing and specify in separate sections:

1. the court, time and place of pronouncement of the judgment;

2. the parties and their attorneys or assistants and the defence counsel of the defendant;

3. the ultimate order of the court;

4. the parties' demands and the circumstances upon which they are founded; and

5. the reasoning in support of the judgment, including a statement of what has been proved in the action.

A judgment rendered by an appellate court shall, to the necessary extent, describe the judgment of the court below.

If a party may appeal from a judgment, it shall state the steps he must take to do so. Further instructions in a judgment of a court of appeals are prescribed in chapter 54, section 14. (SFS 1969:101)

**Section 6**

If the defendant has acknowledged his guilt and a sanction other than imprisonment or of imprisonment for at most six months is imposed, the judgment may be rendered in simplified form. A judgment by an appellate court confirming the judgment of a court below may also be rendered in simplified form.

If a private claim in consequence of an offence is made in the case, the provisions in the first sentence of the first paragraph apply only if the defendant acknowledges the claim or if the court deems the matter to be manifest. (SFS 1981:1093)

**Section 7**

Before rendering judgment the court shall meet to deliberate. When a panel of lay judges sits in the court, the chairman or, if the action has been prepared by another judge learned in law, the latter shall explain the subject matter of the case and the applicable legal rules to the panel.

When a main hearing has been held, deliberation shall take place either on the same day or the next working weekday and, if possible, the judgment shall be determined and read out in court prior to adjournment. When additional time is unavoidably required for the determination or writing of the judgment, the court may decide upon an extension; unless there is an extraordinary impediment, however, the judgment shall be composed in writing and pronounced, if the defendant is detained, within one week or, otherwise, within two weeks of the conclusion of the hearings. If the judgment is not read out in open court at the main hearing, it shall be read at another session of the court or held accessible to the public at the court's clerical office; at the conclusion of the main hearing a notice of the time and manner of pronouncement of judgment shall be given.

When actions are adjudicated without a main hearing, the deliberation shall take place and the judgment be determined, composed in writing and pronounced as soon as possible. Pronouncement shall occur by making the judgment accessible at the court's clerical office. A notice of the time of pronouncement shall be sent to the parties at the latest on the same day as the pronouncement.

Pronouncement of a judgment in open court may occur by reporting the reasoning in support of the judgment and the ultimate order and by notifying the parties of the means by which the judgment may be attacked.

If there has been a divergent opinion, it shall be notified to the parties at the same time and in the same manner as the judgment.

When an action has been adjudicated, a written notice of its outcome shall be delivered as soon as possible to the defendant. (SFS 1976:560)

**Section 8**

Every judgment shall be separately drawn up and signed by the judges learned in law participating in the adjudication.

The judgments rendered by a court during a calendar year, filed and numbered consequtively by date of issuance, shall be put together to compose a judgment book.

**Section 9**

Upon the expiration of the time for ordinary means of appeal the issue of criminal liability of the defendant for the act to which the judgment relates may not be taken up again for adjudication.

As to change and concurrence of criminal sanctions, extraordinary means of attack, and transfer of prosecution to a foreign state in certain cases, the specific provisions thereon shall apply. (SFS 1976:21)

**Section 10**

The provisions of sections 2 and 7 concerning judgments shall correspondingly apply to final orders. Unless otherwise prescribed, the provisions in sections 5 and 8 shall also apply to such orders if required by the nature of the issue. When a final order is rendered in conjunction with the judgment, it shall be included in the judgment.

If a party may appeal from a final order or apply for reinstatement, the order shall provide instructions as to the steps he must take to do so. Further instructions to be included in a final order of a court of appeals are prescribed in chapter 54, section 14. (SFS 1982:1123)

**Section 11**

An order other than a final order shall state, to the extent necessary, the reasoning supporting the determination.

If a person who desires to appeal from an order rendered during the proceedings must take formal exception thereto, he shall be notified to that effect. If an appeal from such an order must be brought independently, the court shall also give an instruction to that effect. Anyone desiring to appeal from the order may request of the court further instructions concerning the taking of an appeal.

When an order other than a final order is rendered in conjunction with a judgment or final order, it shall be included in the judgment or final order. If an appeal from the order must be brought independently, the court shall furnish instructions as to the steps necessary to perfect an appeal.

Further instructions to be included in the orders of courts of appeals are prescribed in chapter 54, section 14.

**Section 12**

Orders rendered during the proceedings which may not be challenged separately shall be immediately effective. The same applies to orders by which the court

1. has dismissed an attorney, assistant or defence counsel,

2. decided the compensation or advance payment out of public funds to an injured person or to an assistant, defence counsel, witness, expert or any person other than the parties,

3. decided an issue of detention or a measure stated in chapters 25–28,

4. appointed as defence counsel a person other than proposed by the party, or

5. decided in a case other than referred to in 2 or 4 concerning legal aid under the Legal Aid Act (1972:429), but not an order to repay to the Treasury the cost of legal aid.

For cause, in an order to a party or third person to produce documentary evidence or to make accessible an object for view or inspection, the court may direct that the order be made immediately effective. When reason exists, the court shall prescribe that security be furnished for damages for which the party may be liable if the order is amended.

A special direction to the effect that a judgment or order shall be immediately effective shall govern. (SFS 1981:828)

**Section 13**

When the court finds, as a result of a complaint or otherwise, that a judgment or order is evidently incorrect owing to an error in transcription, calculation, or any other similar oversight, after affording the parties an opportunity to be heard, the court shall direct amendment of the judgment or order.

Amendments shall be entered directly on the original judgment or order, or, if the order is included in a protocol, upon the protocol and, if possible, upon all copies of the judgment or order together with a notation of the date of the entry.

**Section 14**

Repealed by SFS 1976:567.

## Chapter 31

### Litigation Costs

#### Section 1

In a case presented by a prosecutor, if the defendant is sentenced for the offence, he shall repay the Treasury the sums paid out of public funds by order of the court for his appearance in the court during the preliminary investigation, to Witnesses or experts, or otherwise for evidence during the preliminary investigation or the procedings, and to his defence counsel as compensation; he shall also reimburse the Treasury for the expenses of taking him in custody to the court. However, the defendant shall not be liable for expenses not reasonably required for the inquiry, nor for expenses caused by the carelessness or oversight of a person other than the defendant, his attorney or a defence counsel appointed by him. Nor, in a case other than stated in section 4, first paragraph, shall he be obliged to pay more than the maximum amount for which he would be liable for public legal aid under the Legal Aid Act.

If the amount that the defendant would be liable to pay in compensation is below a given limit determined by the Government, no liability shall be imposed.

What the defendant shall repay in accordance with the first paragraph may be adjusted or remitted if cause exists having regard to his guilt or to his personal and financial circumstances.

If the amount that the defendant would be liable to pay in compensation is below a given limit determined by the Government, no liability shall be imposed. (SFS 1983:154)

#### Section 2

In a case presented by a prosecutor in which the defendant is acquitted, or if the prosecution instituted by the prosecutor is dismissed without reaching the merits or written off, the court may award him compensation out of public funds for his expenses for defence counsel, advice under the Legal Aid Act (1972:429), witnesses or experts, evidence of any other kind during the preliminary investigation or the proceedings, service, and copies of protocols or the like, provided that the expenses were reasonably required to protect his rights; he may also receive compensation for his appearance before the court.

Compensation for appearance of the defendant shall be paid as provided for a defendant enjoying legal aid. (SFS 1983:920)

### Section 3

If a prosecutor is found to have instituted a prosecution without cause, he may be ordered to reimburse the Treasury for the costs stated in section 1, as well as for the compensation awarded the defendant pursuant to section 2.

If an injured person has made an accusation or has otherwise instigated the prosecution without cause, liability to provide compensation for costs may also be placed upon him to the extent found reasonable.

### Section 4

In an action brought by the prosecutor, if the defendant's failure to appear before the court, or to comply with a court direction, or his presentation of an allegation or a defence that he knew or should have known to be without merit, or carelessness or oversight in other respects, has occasioned adjournment of the proceedings or has otherwise caused expenses for the Treasury, the defendant shall be liable to furnish compensation for such expenses, regardless of how costs in general are to be distributed.

The aforesaid shall correspondingly apply if, by carelessness or oversight, the prosecutor, the injured person, or a public defence counsel has caused expenses for the Crown or the defendant.

### Section 5

If pursuant to this chapter a private party must furnish compensation for litigation expenses in whole or in part, and it is found that the legal representative of the party, or the party's attorney or assistant, or a defence counsel privately appointed by him, has caused the costs by conduct described in section 3, second paragraph, or by such carelessness or oversight as is referred to in section 4, the court, even if not requested to do so, may impose joint liability for costs upon the party and his legal representative, attorney, assistant, or defence counsel.

### Section 6

When several persons are sentenced for joint commission of the same offence, or for offences connected with each other, or when several injured persons or the prosecutor and the injured person shall furnish compensation for litigation expenses, they shall be jointly and severally liable for the expenses. However, to the extent that items of expenses are chargeable to a portion of the action involving only one of these persons, or that one of them has occasioned items of expenses by such carelessness or oversight as is described in section 4, only the one who occasioned the expenses shall be charged.

When a person is liable to furnish compensation for litigation costs together with a party pursuant to section 5, they shall be liable for the costs jointly and severally. (SFS 1948:453)

**Section 7**

When two or more persons are jointly and severally liable for litigation costs, on the request of one of them, the court, in view of the particular circumstances, may specify the portion of the expenses that each shall ultimately bear, or authorize complete indemnification of one or more by the other.

**Section 8**

When a preliminary investigation has been discontinued, or otherwise has not resulted in a prosecution, the provisions in sections 2 to 7 shall correspondingly apply to costs incurred during the investigation; the Treasury may not be ordered to furnish compensation for such costs unless the investigation has been initiated without cause or there is otherwise extraordinary cause for it.

When the injured person, pursuant to chapter 20, section 9, has taken over a prosecution withdrawn by the prosecutor, the provisions in section 1 to 7 shall govern as to costs incurred prior to the take-over.

**Section 9**

If a prosecutor seeks an order that the defendant furnish compensation for litigation costs, or if a defendant wishes to be compensated for such costs, he shall make a demand for, and present a list of his expenses to the court before the termination of the proceedings. If he fails to do so, he forfeits his right to seek reimbursement for expenses incurred in that court. The court shall determine on its own motion whether disbursements paid out of public funds in accordance with court orders shall be reimbursed by the defendant, or by any other person, or rest with the Treasury. Matters referred to in section 3 shall also be tried by the court on its own motion.

When finally disposing of the action the court shall simultaneously rule upon the litigation costs.

If a preliminary investigation has been commenced but has not resulted in a prosecution, and the suspect desires to claim compensation for expenses during the investigation, or if a question as to compensation of the Treasury for such expenses is raised, an application for such compensation shall be made to the court. (SFS 1972:430)

**Section 10**

The determination concerning liability to provide compensation for litigation costs incurred in an appellate court in an appeal from a court below shall be based upon the outcome of the action in the appellate court. A judgment by an appellate court shall be considered condemnatory only when the defendant is sentenced to a sanction more severe than the one to which the court below had sentenced him or, if he was acquitted in the court below, when he is found guilty of the offence by the appellate court, or when an appeal by the defendant does not result in a change in the judgment of the court below. The provisions in section 3 are applicable when the prosecutor has appealed to a higher court without cause.

As to liability for expenses incurred in a higher court when the proceeding concerns an issue separately appealed to that court, the provisions in this chapter as to actions instituted in lower courts shall correspondingly apply.

If an action is referred back to a court below, the issue of costs incurred in the higher court shall be determined by the court below after it rehears the case. (SFS 1964:166)

**Section 11**

As to litigation costs in an action brought solely by an injured person, the provisions in chapter 18 shall apply to the extent relevant.

As to the liability of the defendant to reimburse the Treasury for costs of defence counsel and other legal aid awarded to him, however, section 1, first paragraph, last sentence, and second and third paragraphs, of this chapter shall correspondingly apply.

As to the liability of an injured person, in an action in which he supports the public prosecution or otherwise joins with the prosecutor, or in which the latter has appeared on behalf of the injured person, to pay litigation costs, and his right to reimbursement for such costs, the provisions in sections 3 and 4 and in chapter 18, section 12, shall apply. (SFS 1983:920)

**Section 12**

If provisions on litigation costs contained in any law or decree are inconsistent with the regulations contained in this chapter, the former shall govern.

# III Regulations for both Civil and Criminal Cases

## Chapter 32

### Time Regulations and Legal Excuse

#### Section 1

When a party or any other person, pursuant to court order, is required to appear before the court or to perform any other act in the proceedings, he shall be given reasonable time to comply with the court's directive.

#### Section 2

If a summons, a petition for regular or limited appeal, or a review petition, is to be served by a party and if, at the time the court takes up the case, there is neither proof of service filed within the time and in the manner specified, nor has the adverse party appeared or filed an answer, rejoinder or declaration, the action, appeal or petition shall be dismissed. A note to this effect shall be included in the court's directive concerning the service. (SFS 1970:429)

#### Section 3

When a party or any other person is required by court order to appear in court or to perform any other act in the course of the proceedings, and it is found that he has not been afforded adequate time, or when order grounds furnish cause for the extension of a time prescribed by the court, the court shall specify a new time.

#### Section 4

When a hearing has been scheduled but has not yet been held, if the court finds that a circumstance exists which can be assumed to impede the holding of the hearing or a sufficiently comprehensive presentation and consideration of the matter scheduled to be heard, the court may direct a new time for the hearing.

When a party has become aware of a circumstance of the kind referred to above, or when a person served with a notice to appear at a hearing finds that he is unable to comply with the court's directive, he shall immediately notify the court thereof.

#### Section 5

When it is of extraordinary importance for the determination of an action that a question sub judice in another court proceeding or in a proceeding of another kind be determined first, or when another impediment to adjudication of considerable duration is encountered, the court may order a stay of proceedings pending removal of the impediment.

### Section 6

If a person who is required by court order to appear in court or to perform any other act in the course of the proceedings fails to comply with the order and there is cause to believe that he has legal excuse, no sanction shall be imposed for the non-compliance, nor shall it expose him to any detriment in the proceeding.

### Section 7

Whenever this Code prescribes a specified time within which a person who wishes to appeal shall take a formal exception, or file a notice of appeal, or observe any other requirement for the perfection of his appeal, and the existence of legal excuse is established prior to the expiration of the prescribed time, the court in which the measure must be taken shall specify a new time.

The same rule shall correspondingly apply to applications for reopening or reinstatement.

### Section 8

Legal excuse exists when a person was impeded from doing what was required of him by reason of a breakdown in the general modes of communication, sickness, or another circumstance that he did not have cause to anticipate or that the court otherwise regards as constituting a valid excuse.

As to a party, legal excuse is also deemed to exist when an attorney retained by him was impeded by a hindrance of the kind mentioned above and the party was unable to commission another attorney within the time available to him.

# Chapter 33

## Party Writings; Service

### Section 1

Applications, notices and other party writings shall state the name of the court and the name and residence of the parties.

A party's first writing shall specify his personal identity number and postal address. It should also state his occupation and telephone number and any other circumstance of importance for service upon him. When a party has retained an attorney, the name and postal address of the attorney shall be stated.

A summons application should also contain particulars of the defendant in the respect stated in the second paragraph.

If a change occurs in any fact or circumstance thus specified by a party, he shall notify the court without delay. (SFS 1973:240)

**Section 2**

When a writing or any other paper filed by a party is to be served, the party must attach to the document a certified copy thereof. If service is to be effected by the court and more than one copy is required to effect the service, the party shall furnish the court with the required number of copies. If the party does not furnish the said copies, the court shall direct the copying of the document at the party's expense.

**Section 3**

Any party writing or other document is deemed files with the court on the day when the document or a note of the prepaid postal despatch in which it is enclosed is received at the court or by a competent official. If the court is specially notified that a telegram to the court has been received at a telegraph office, the telegram is deemed filed at the time when the notification reached a competent official.

If it may be assumed that the document or note of despatch has been delivered to the court's clerical office or set aside by a post office for delivery to the court, it is deemed filed on that day if received by a competent official on the next working weekday.

A telegram or other non-signed communication shall be confirmed by the despatcher by signing of a document if the court so requests. (SFS 1973:240)

**Section 4**

As to service in general, separate provisions apply. (SFS 1970:429)

**Section 5**

A default judgment shall be served by the court only

if it stipulates payment of a claim with preferential right in personal or real property,

if the party demanding the default judgment so request, or

if a party has been granted public legal aid. (SFS 1981:828)

## Section 6

The provisions in sections 5, 12 and 15 of the Service of Documents Act (1970:428) shall not apply to service of a summons in criminal cases.

Nor in civil cases may a summons be served as prescribed in section 12 of the Service of Documents Act unless there is cause to believe that the addressee has fled or is otherwise concealing himself. (SFS 1970:429)

## Section 7

When anyone has filed with the Supreme Court a written notice of the appointment of an attorney authorized to receive service of a summons or other document, service may be made upon the attorney to the extent indicated in the notice.

The notice may be filed only by a person residing within the realm at the time of filing and shall specify the period for which it is effective. This period may not exceed three years. Only a person residing within the realm may be registered as attorney. The postal address of the attorney shall be furnished together with the notice. If the address of the attorney is changed, notice thereof shall be filed.

If an attorney is authorized to receive service on behalf of his principal pursuant to this section, the provisions in sections 5 and 15 of the Service of Documents Act shall not apply to the principal unless service upon the attorney pursuant to section 7 or 12 of the said Act cannot be made. (SFS 1972:147)

## Section 8

If a party who is not residing in the realm has not notified the court of the name of an attorney authorized to accept service on his behalf, the court shall direct the party, upon his first appearance in court, to appoint such an attorney and notify the court thereof. If the party fails to comply with the direction, service upon him may be made by ordinary mail at his last known address. (SFS 1970:429)

## Section 9

If a party writing or other document is not composed in the Swedish language, the court may, if necessary, either direct the party to furnish an attested translation thereof or commission a suitable person to translate the document. If the direction to furnish a translation is not complied with, the document may be disregarded.

A person who has assisted the court in translation shall be entitled to remuneration out of public funds to the extent that the court finds reasonable; in criminal actions instituted by a public prosecutor the remuneration shall be paid by the Treasury. (SFS 1973:240)

### Sections 10–27

Repealed by SFS 1970:429.

## Chapter 34

### Procedural Hindrances

### Section 1

The court shall consider any hindrance to the processing of an action as soon as reason therefor arises.

In the absence of provision to the contrary, the court shall take notice of procedural hindrances on its own motion.

### Section 2

Any party who wishes to assert an objection that the court lacks competence to try the case shall do so when he makes his first appearance in the action. If prevented from presenting the objection at that time by legal excuse, he shall present it as soon as possible after the excuse has ceased to exist. A party who fails to object within the time stated above forfeits his right to raise the objection.

### Section 3

If a party has made a timely objection pursuant to section 2, the court shall issue a separate order thereon as soon as possible. As to an objection based upon any other alleged procedural hindrance, the court shall issue a separate order thereon if the character of the hindrance so requires.

# Part Three

# Evidence

## Chapter 35

### Evidence in General

#### Section 1

After evaluating everything that has occurred in the proceeding in accordance with the dictates of its conscience, the court shall determine what has been proved in the case.

As to the probative effect of certain kinds of evidence, the specific provisions thereon shall govern.

#### Section 2

Proof of a circumstance that is generally known is not required.

Nor is proof required as to legal rules. However, if foreign law is to be applied and its content is not known to the court, the court may request one or both parties to present proof thereof.

#### Section 3

In a case amenable to out of court settlement, if a party admits a certain fact during the proceedings, his admission constitutes full proof against him. If the party withdraws his admission, the court shall determine, in view of the reasons for the withdrawal and other circumstances, the probative effect, if any, of the admission.

In cases other than those mentioned in the first paragraph, the court shall determine with respect to the particular circumstances the evidentiary significance of the admission. (SFS 1958:641)

#### Section 4

If a party fails to respond to a court direction to appear before it or to perform any other procedural act, or refuses to answer a question relevant to the investigation, the court shall determine, in view of all the attending circumstances, the evidentiary significance of the party's behaviour.

**Section 5**

With respect to the extent of damages, if full proof cannot be presented at all or only with difficulty, the court shall award a reasonable amount.

**Section 6**

Presentation of evidence is the responsibility of the parties. If it is found necessary, the court may also arrange for presentation of evidence on its own motion. In civil cases amenable to out of court settlement, and in criminal cases concerning offences not within the domain of public prosecution, however, the court may not examine a witness unless a party proposes that the witness be heard or the witness was previously examined on request of a party, nor may the court direct the production of documentary evidence except on request of a party.

**Section 7**

If the court finds that a circumstance which a party desires to prove is without importance in the case, or that a claimed item of evidence is unnecessary or evidently would be of no probative effect, the court shall reject that proof. The court may also reject an offered item of evidence if the proof may be presented in another way with considerably less trouble or cost.

**Section 8**

If a main hearing is held, the evidence is to be taken at that hearing unless, in accordance with special provisions thereon, it may be taken outside the main hearing. If a main hearing is not held, or if evidence is otherwise to be taken outside that hearing, the evidence may be taken at the court in which the action is pending or at another court.

**Section 9**

When the proof is to be taken outside a main hearing, a notice to appear shall be served on the parties. In a criminal case, if the defendant is under arrest or in detention, and his appearance is found necessary, the court shall direct that he be brought before it. If a party fails to appear, the evidence may nonetheless be taken.

**Section 10**

If the court in which an action is pending directs that evidence be taken by another court within the realm, the court in which the action is pending shall present a request to the court designated to take the evidence, stating therein a brief account of the matter in controversy, the evidence sought, and the circumstance to be proved thereby. The case file shall be attached to the request if transmission of the file is found appropriate and there is no impediment to its dispatch from the court in which the action is pending.

**Section 11**

A court requested to take evidence for use in an action pending before another court shall fix a time and place for the proof-taking. At the hearing to execute the request, the authority of the court is the same as would exist if the action were pending before it.

The record from the proof-taking, together with all the documents forwarded to the court that took the evidence or otherwise relating to the matter, shall be sent to the court in which the action is pending.

**Section 12**

As to proof-taking in foreign countries special provisions have been enacted.

**Section 13**

Evidence taken outside the main hearing shall be re-taken at the main hearing if the evidence is found to be of importance in the case, and the impediment to its presentation at the main hearing no longer exists.

In a case appealed to a higher court, if a court below took the testimony of a witness or expert, or of a party under truth affirmation, or held a view of the locus in quo, re-presentation of the evidence in the higher court is not necessary unless the court finds that renewal of the proof-taking is of importance for the investigation, or a party requests such re-presentation and the requested renewal is not considered by the court to lack importance. In the Supreme Court, however, such evidence may be re-taken only for extraordinary cause.

When evidence is not re-taken, it shall be brought forward from the record and other documents concerning the proof-taking.

**Section 14**

Neither a written statement made by a person by reason of a pending or contemplated proceeding, nor a recorded account of a statement given to a prosecutor or police authority, or otherwise made out of court by reason of a pending or contemplated proceeding, may be admitted as proof unless admission of the statement or recorded account is specifically authorized by law, or the court finds admission justified based upon special circumstances.

## Chapter 36

### Witnesses

#### Section 1

Anyone who is not a party in the case may be heard as witness. In a criminal case, however, the injured party may not be heard as witness even if he presents no claim in the case.

Nor, in a criminal case, may a person be heard as witness who has been prosecuted for an offence to which the hearing relates nor for any other offence directly connected with that offence.

The provisions of the second paragraph concerning a person prosecuted shall apply also to a person who, for an offence as referred to therein

1. is reasonably suspected and has been notified of the suspicion as stated in chapter 23, section 18,

2. has been given an order of summary punishment by fine or been notified of a breach-of-regulations fine or been subjected to disciplinary punishment by a military officer, or

3. has not been prosecuted consequent on a decision pursuant to regulations governing waiver of prosecution or special examination of grounds for prosecution.

If a person as referred to in the second or third paragraph is to be heard in a trial not involving prosecution against himself, the provisions of chapter 31, section 4, chapter 45, section 15, and chapter 46, shall rule as regards summons to proceedings and sanction for non-appearance and as regards the interrogation. The right to compensation for appearance at proceedings is governed by the provisions of chapter 36, sections 24 and 25. (SFS 1984:131)

#### Section 2

If a member of the court is called as a witness, he shall consider on his oath as a judge whether he knows anything that might be informative in the action. If he finds that he does, he may testify as a witness.

#### Section 3

A spouse, former spouse, relative by blood or by marriage in direct lineal ascent or descent, or brother or sister of a party, or a person so related to a party by marriage that one of them is or has been married to a brother or sister of the other, or similarly related to a party, is not obliged to testify.

A person correspondingly related to a party's legal representative may not avoid the duty to testify by reason of that relationship. (SFS 1973:240)

### Section 4

If testimony is sought from a person under the age of fifteen years, or suffering from mental disease, feeble-mindedness, or any other mental disturbance, the court shall determine in accordance with the particular circumstances whether he may be heard as a witness.

### Section 5

No person who, pursuant to chapter 2, section 1 or 2, or chapter 3, section 1, of the Official Secrets Act (1980:100) or a regulation referred to in any of these statutory provisions, has a duty to maintain secrecy, may not testify as witness thereon without permission of the authority concerned.

Nor may an advocate, physician, dentist, midwife, nurse, official at a family advice bureau run by a local or county council, parish or ecclesiastical congregation, or an assistant to any such person, be examined concerning matters entrusted to, or found out by, him in his professional capacity, unless the examination is authorized by law or consented to by the person for whose benefit the duty of secrecy is imposed.

No attorney, assistant or defence counsel may testify as witness concerning matters entrusted to him in the performance of his commission unless his client consents to the disclosure.

Notwithstanding the provisions in the second and third paragraphs, persons other than a defence counsel are obliged to testify in a criminal prosecution for an offence punishable by a minimum sentence of two years imprisonment.

As to the duty to observe secrecy of a minister of the Swedish state church, special provisions have been enacted. No minister of a congregation other than the state church, nor anyone having a corresponding standing in such a congregation, may testify as witness concerning matters made known to him in a private confession or in a conversation for the care of souls.

A person who has a duty to observe secrecy under the provisions of chapter 3, section 3, of the Freedom of the Press Act, section 9 of the Radio Responsibility Act (1966:756), section 1 of the Act concerning Responsibility in Community Radio Trials (1982:460) or section 11 of the Act concerning Responsibility for Radio and Cassette Newspapers (1982:521) may testify as witness concerning matters for which a duty of secrecy is imposed only to the extent allowed by the said sections. (SFS 1982:522)

## Section 6

A witness may decline to testify concerning a circumstance that might reveal that he, or a person related to him as stated in section 3, has committed a crime or a dishonorable act. Further, a witness may refrain from giving testimony that would involve disclosure of a trade secret, unless there is extraordinary cause for examining the witness on the matter.

## Section 7

If the person whose testimony is sought is present in the court, he is obliged to testify immediately. If he is not present, he shall be served with a notice to appear.

The notice to appear shall state the parties, the case, and the time and place for the appearance of the witness; it shall also contain a summary description of the matter upon which testimony is sought. Further, the notice shall refer the witness to the provisions in sections 20, 23 and 25.

## Section 8

The court may instruct a witness, before his appearance to testify, to refresh his memory on the subject of his testimony by examining accessible account-books, notes or other documents or by inspecting a place or an object if this can be done without considerable inconvenience to the witness.

If, pursuant to chapter 3, section 3, 5, of the Freedom of the Press Act, section 9, first paragraph, 5, of the Radio Responsibility Act (1966:756) or section 11, 5, of the Act concerning Responsibility for Radio and Cassette Newspapers (1982:521), the court is to consider whether anyone who has the duty to maintain secrecy concerning information there referred to may nevertheless testify as witness thereon, the court shall first, unless special reasons dictate otherwise, procure a statement from the enterprise from which the person acquired knowledge thereof. (SFS 1982:522)

## Section 9

In the absence of special cause for his attendance, a witness may not observe the proceedings in the case prior to his testimony.

When there are two or more witnesses in the case, each shall testify separately. If their separate testimony is ambiguous or conflicting, or if special cause otherwise exists, witnesses may be examined confronting each other.

**Section 10**

Before hearing a witness, the court shall ask him to state his full name, age, occupation and residence and attempt to ascertain whether he has a relationship to any of the parties, or to the matter in controversy, that might be of importance in evaluating the reliability of his testimony, or whether any other circumstance exists that may be of importance in that respect.

Any witness related to a party as stated in section 3 shall be advised that he is under no obligation to testify.

**Section 11**

Before giving testimony the witness shall take this oath:

"I (name) promise and assure upon my faith and honour that I shall speak the whole truth and will not conceal, add or change anything." (SFS 1975:1288)

**Section 12**

Repealed by SFS 1975:1288.

**Section 13**

An oath may not be taken by

1. a person under the age of fifteen years; or

2. a person who, owing to mental disease, feeble-mindedness or any other mental disturbance is found to lack insight into the importance of the oath.

Nor in criminal cases may an oath be taken by a person related to the defendant as stated in section 3. (SFS 1975:1288)

**Section 14**

Before hearing a witness, the court shall warn him of his duty to tell the truth and, when he has taken the oath, shall remind him of its significance. When there in cause therefor, the witness shall also be reminded of the provisions in sections 5 and 6. (SFS 1975:1288)

**Section 15**

Each witness shall take the oath separately.

A witness re-testifying in the case may be examined on the oath taken previously; the witness shall be reminded by the court that this oath continues in effect. (SFS 1975:1288)

## Section 16

A witness shall give his testimony orally. A written affidavit may not be quoted; however, the witness may be permitted to support his memory with written notes made at the time of the event in question.

During the examination, a written account of statements previously made by the witness before a court, public prosecutor, or police authority may be read only when the witness departs from his earlier statement, or declares himself unable or unwilling to testify.

## Section 17

Witnesses shall be examined by the court. With the consent of the court, however, a witness may be examined by the parties, initially by the party on whose behalf the witness has been called and subsequently by the adverse party.

The witness should be invited to give his testimony in continuous sequence without interruption. After he had given his account of the matter on which his testimony was sought, the court and the parties may put questions to him. If it is not evident from the testimony, the witness should be questioned as to the manner in which he obtained knowledge of the matters on which he has expressed himself.

In the absence of special cause, questions inviting a specific answer by their content or form, or by the way they are presented, may not be put to a witness. The court shall exclude questions that are plainly irrelevant, confusing, or otherwise inappropriate.

## Section 18

If there is cause to believe that, in the presence of a party, a witness, through fear or otherwise, is likely to be inhibited from telling the truth unreservedly, or if a party hinders the witness from testifying by interrupting the witness or otherwise, the court may exclude the party from the courtroom during the examination.

Upon the return of the party, the testimony shall be read to him; thereafter the party may question the witness.

## Section 19

If a witness is unable to appear at the main hearing because of illness, sojourn at a distant place, or other cause, or if it is found that the presence of the witness would occasion unreasonable expenses or special inconvenience, the court may order examination of the witness outside the main hearing. If a witness cannot appear because of illness, he shall be examined at the place in which he sojours.

**Section 20**

A witness who fails to respond to a notice to appear shall be fined. If the case is postponed to a later date, the witness may be directed on penalty of fine to appear on that date. If he again fails to appear, the conditional fine or, when no such fine was directed, an ordinary fine shall be imposed upon him.

On court order, a witness who fails to appear at the outset of a hearing in the case may be brought to that hearing in custody. If the witness is not brought to that hearing in custody, or directed on penalty of fine to appear on a later date, the court may order that he be brought before it in custody on a later date. When a witness is brought to a hearing in custody, neither an ordinary nor a conditional fine may be imposed for his failure to appear at the inception of that hearing.

**Section 21**

If a witness, without valid reason, refuses to take an oath or to testify, respond to a particular question or obey an order pursuant to section 8, the court shall order the witness to perform his duty on penalty of fine and, if the witness persists in his refusal, on penalty of detention. A witness so detained may not be held in custody longer than three months and in no instance beyond the time when the court dissociates itself from the case. A witness taken into custody shall appear before the court at least once every two weeks. (SFS 1975:1288)

**Section 22**

As to the witnesses referred to in section 13, first paragraph, the provisions in sections 20 and 21 shall not apply; however, such a witness may be brought to the court in custody.

If the person who sought the testimony of a witness disclaims examination of him, or if the issue of his examination is otherwise dropped, no punishment or coercive measure under section 20 or 21 may be imposed upon the witness.

**Section 23**

If a witness is liable for negligence or contumacy as stated in section 20 or 21, and a party occasions litigation costs thereby, the court, even if not requested to do so, may order the witness to furnish compensation for such costs to the extent found reasonable. Further, if a party was ordered by the court to compensate his adversary for such costs, upon payment, the party may claim reimbursement from the witness to the extent of the sum ordered by the court to be paid by the witness.

The prescriptions above as to the liability of a witness to reimburse a party for expenses shall correspondingly apply to expenses paid out of public funds.

**Section 24**

A witness is entitled to compensation as stated below.

The compensation of a witness called by a private party shall be paid by the party. In civil cases amenable to out of court settlement and in criminal prosecutions for offences that do not fall within the domain of public prosecution, the compensation of witnesses called by the court on its own motion shall be paid by the parties jointly and severally. In all other cases the compensation shall be paid out of public funds.

Compensation paid by a party shall include reimbursement of necessary expenses for travel and maintenance, and for loss of time, in an amount deemed reasonable by the court. Compensation paid out of public funds shall be determined by the court pursuant to regulations issued by the Government. (SFS 1974:573)

**Section 25**

Anyone called as witness is entitled to receive advance payment for travel and maintenance expenses. The advance shall be paid by the party or parties who shall reimburse the witness pursuant to section 24. The amount of the advance is determined by the court.

If a party who is obliged to pay a witness in advance fails to pay the advance when requested to do so, the party may not later request examination of the witness if this would cause postponement of the proceedings in the case.

Further regulations concerning advance payments are issued by the Government. (SFS 1974:573)

## Chapter 37

### Examination of Parties under Truth Affirmation

**Section 1**

For the purpose of obtaining proof in civil actions, one or both parties may be examined under truth affirmation.

A party may request examination of himself or of his adversary under truth affirmation.

**Section 2**

A person who may not take a witness oath pursuant to chapter 36, section 13, first paragraph, may not be examined under truth affirmation.

### Section 3

Before testifying, a party shall take this affirmation:

"I (name) promise and assure on my honour and conscience that I will speak the whole truth and will not conceal, add, or change anything."

After a party has taken the affirmation, the court shall remind him of its significance.

### Section 4

If there is an extraordinary impediment to the presence of a party at the main hearing, the court may order examination of the party outside the main hearing. If a party cannot appear because of illness, he may be examined at the place in which he sojourns.

### Section 5

As to the examination of parties under truth affirmation in other respects, the provisions in chapter 36, sections 5 and 6, section 7, first paragraph, section 8, second paragraph, and sections 15–18, concerning examination of witnesses shall correspondingly apply. (SFS 1977:1020)

# Chapter 38

## Documentary Evidence

### Section 1

Documents presented as proof should be produced in the original. However, a certified copy may be produced if found sufficient, or if the original is not obtainable.

If a document contains information which the possessor is either not entitled or not obliged to disclose pursuant to section 2, or which otherwise should not be disclosed, the possessor may produce, in lieu of the document, a certified excerpt therefrom.

### Section 2

Anyone possessing a document that can be assumed to be of importance as proof is obliged to produce it; however, in criminal cases, such an obligation is not imposed upon the suspect or upon any person related to him as stated in chapter 36, section 3.

Neither a party, nor any person related to him as stated above, is obliged to produce written communications between the party and such a related person, or between such related persons. Neither a public official, nor any other person referred to in chapter 36, section 5, may produce a document if it can be assumed that its content is such that he may not testify as a witness thereto; when the document is possessed by the party for whose benefit an obligation of secrecy is imposed, the party is not obliged to produce the document. The provision in chapter 36, section 6, as to the privilege of a witness to refuse to testify shall correspondingly apply to the possessor of a document, provided that the content of the document is such as is referred to in the said section.

The obligation to produce documents does not extend to memory notes, or to any other like notes prepared exclusively for private use, unless extraordinary cause exists for their production.

**Section 3**

If a possessor of a document, based upon a legal relationship between himself and a party, or as otherwise prescribed by law, is obliged to surrender the document or to allow another to inspect it, this obligation shall also apply to the production of the document in a pending action.

**Section 4**

When anyone is obliged to produce a document as proof, the court may direct him to produce it. The person against whom the directive should be addressed shall be given an opportunity to present any objection he may have to the production. For resolution of an issue so raised, an examination of the person from whom production is sought may be held in accordance with the provisions in chapter 36 and 37, and other proof may be taken.

**Section 5**

A directive for the production of a document shall state the place and manner of production. The person obliged to produce the document may be compelled to perform his duty under penalty of fine. If it appears more suitable, the court may order that the document be obtained and made accessible by an execution officer.

**Section 6**

If an extraordinary impediment to the production of a document at the main hearing is encountered, the court may order that the proof be taken outside the main hearing.

**Section 7**

Anyone other than a party who has produced a document on the request of a party or the court is entitled to compensation for his expenses and inconvenience in an amount found reasonable by the court.

When the production has been requested by a private party, the compensation shall be paid by the party. Otherwise the compensation shall be paid out of public funds.

### Section 8

If a public document may be assumed to be important as evidence, the court may direct that the document be furnished.

The first paragraph does not apply to

1. a document containing particulars subject to secrecy pursuant to chapter 2, section 1 or 2, or chapter 3, section 1, of the Official Secrets Act (1980:100) or to a regulation referred to in any of these statutory provisions, unless the authority which has to examine an issue of surrender of documents has given its consent thereto;

2. a document the contents of which are such that anyone who has been concerned therewith, as stated in chapter 36, section 5, second, third, fourth or sixth paragraph, may not be examined thereon;

3. a document the production of which would disclose a trade secret, except for special cause. (SFS 1980:101)

### Section 9

If provisions which differ from those prescribed in sections 1–8 have been issued concerning the obligation to produce a document, they shall apply. (SFS 1980:101)

## Chapter 39

### Views

### Section 1

For the examination of immovable property, or of objects which cannot be brought conveniently to the courtroom, or of the scene of a special occurrence, the court may hold a view at the locus in quo.

Trade secrets may not be revealed at a view unless extraordinary cause justifies disclosure.

### Section 2

If it is of extraordinary importance, by reason of the condition of the object, or for other reasons, that a view occur prior to the main hearing, or if a view cannot conveniently be held at the main hearing, the court may order that it take place outside the main hearing.

### Section 3

When a view is held outside the main hearing, other proof may be taken thereat if found necessary to accomplish the purpose of the view.

### Section 4

The cost for holding a view, except in cases referred to in chapter 41, shall be paid by the Treasury. (SFS 1969:244)

### Section 5

Anyone possessing an object that can conveniently be brought to the courtroom, and that can be assumed to be of importance as proof, is obliged to make the object accessible for inspection at a view; in criminal cases, however, such an obligation is not imposed upon the suspect or upon any person related to him as stated in chapter 36, section 3. The provision in chapter 36, section 6, as to the privilege of a witness to refuse to testify shall correspondingly apply to the privilege of a party, or any other person, to refuse to make an object available for inspection at a view. As to the duty to produce a document for inspection at a view the provisions in chapter 38, section 2, shall apply.

The provisions in chapter 38, sections 3–9, shall correspondingly apply to objects and documents which are to be made available for inspection at a view. (SFS 1980:101)

## Chapter 40

### Experts

### Section 1

If, for the determination of a matter, the appraisal of which requires special professional knowledge, it is found necessary to call upon an expert, the court may obtain an opinion on the matter from a public authority or officer, or from any person specially licensed to furnish opinions on the matter, or commission one or more persons known for their integrity and their knowledge of the subject to deliver an opinion.

### Section 2

A person whose relationship to a party or to the matter in controversy is such as to cast doubt upon his reliability may not be called as an expert.

### Section 3

Before appointing an expert, the court should invite the parties to state their views thereon. If the parties agree upon an expert, he shall be used, provided that he is found suitable, and that there is no impediment to his appointment; however, the court may commission an additional expert.

### Section 4

Except for persons who in their official capacity are obliged to assist as experts and those specially licensed to furnish opinions, no person is required to perform the commission of an expert unless he voluntarily undertakes to do so. A person who has undertaken such a commission may not avoid its performance without valid excuse. No expert, however, is obliged to disclose a trade secret, unless extraordinary cause requires that he give an opinion which would entail such disclosure.

### Section 5

When, for the elucidation of a circumstance of importance for the task of the expert, a party or any other person should be examined or any other investigation occur in court prior to the main hearing, the court may so order. The provisions on proof-taking outside a main hearing shall correspondingly apply.

If inspection is required of immovable property, objects that cannot be moved conveniently, or the scene of a special occurrence, the court may direct that the expert make an on the site inspection. At such inspections trade secrets may not be disclosed unless the court finds that there is extraordinary cause for such disclosure.

The court may direct that objects which, pursuant to chapter 39, section 5, a possessor is obliged to produce in court, shall be made available to the expert for inspection.

### Section 6

If the presence of the parties at an expert's inspection is found appropriate, the court may direct that they shall be notified by the expert to attend the inspection. If a party has been so notified, his absence does not constitute an impediment to the occurrence of the inspection.

A record shall be made at the inspection which shall state the persons present and what occurred thereat.

**Section 7**

As to the reports of public authorities, or officers, or of persons specially licensed to furnish opinions, the specific provisions thereon and, in other respects, established practice shall govern.

Unless the court prescribes otherwise, any other expert shall submit a written opinion. The court shall direct the expert to submit the report within a fixed period.

The report shall state the reasoning and circumstances upon which the conclusion in the report are founded.

After the report is filed with the court, it shall be held accessible to the parties.

**Section 8**

An expert who has submitted a written opinion shall also be examined orally, if a party requests it, unless examination of the expert is plainly without importance, or if the court finds it necessary. As to a report obtained from a central administrative board, an academy, or any other official society, neither the board or society nor any person who participated in preparing the report may be examined orally, unless such examination is found unavoidably necessary; if several persons have cooperated in preparing the report, only one representative of each view expressed in the report may be called.

**Section 9**

Prior to testifying in the court an expert who is examined orally shall take this oath:

"I (name) promise and assure on my faith and honour that I will perform the expert task assigned to me to the best of my ability".

If the expert has submitted a report prior to his examination, the oath shall be adjusted accordingly.

After the expert has taken the oath, the court shall remind him of its significance. (SFS 1975:1288)

**Section 10**

When an expert is examined orally, the examination is conducted by the court. However, with the consent of the court, an expert may be examined by the parties. The court and the parties may put questions to the expert.

The court shall exclude questions that are plainly irrelevant, confusing, or otherwise inappropriate.

If the expert has submitted a written opinion, and the court finds it suitable, all or part of the opinion may be read aloud.

### Section 11

The provisions in chapter 36, section 7, first paragraph, section 9, second paragraph, and sections 15, 18 and 19 concerning witnesses shall correspondingly apply to experts.

### Section 12

If a person who has undertaken to serve as an expert fails to submit his written opinion within the fixed period without a valid excuse, the court may order him to submit the report on penalty of fine.

### Section 13

If an expert served with a notice to appear for examination does not appear, he shall be fined. If the case is postponed to a later date, the expert may be directed to appear on that date on penalty of fine.

### Section 14

If an expert refuses without valid reason to take an oath or to testify or respond to a question, the court shall direct him to perform his duty on penalty of fine. (SFS 1975:1288)

### Section 15

If the commission of an expert is withdrawn or otherwise discontinued, he may not thereafter be subjected to punishment or coercive measures under sections 12, 13 or 14.

### Section 16

If an expert is liable for negligence or contumacy as stated in sections 12, 13 or 14, and a party incurs litigation costs thereby, the court, even if not requested to do so, may order the expert to furnish compensation for such costs to the extent found reasonable. Further, if a party was ordered by the court to compensate his adversary for such costs, upon payment, the party may claim reimbursement from the expert to the extent of the sum ordered by the court to be paid by the expert.

The prescriptions as to the liability of an expert to reimburse a party for expenses shall correspondingly apply to expenses paid out of public funds.

### Section 17

When a report has been submitted by a public authority or officer, or by a person specially licensed to furnish opinions, compensation shall be paid only to the extent special provisions so prescribe. Any other expert is entitled to compensation for expenses accruing in the execution of his duties, and for expenditure of his time and effort in an amount found reasonable by the court.

In civil cases amenable to out of court settlement, and in prosecutions for offences not within the domain of public prosecution, the compensation shall be paid by the parties jointly and severally or, if only one of the parties has requested employment of the expert, by that party alone. In all other cases, the compensation shall be paid out of public funds.

### Section 18

An expert is entitled to advance payment of his compensation in an amount found reasonable by the court. The advance payment shall be made by the party, or parties, or out of private funds, as stated in section 17.

Further regulations concerning advance payments are issued by the Government. (SFS 1974:573)

### Section 19

As to experts not appointed by the court, but claimed by a party, the provisions in sections 7 and 8 shall apply to the extent relevant.

In other respects, when such an expert is orally examined, the provisions concerning witnesses shall apply; however, if the court finds it suitable, all or part of a written opinion may be read aloud.

### Section 20

Specific regulations prescribed by law or decree on the examination of experts in particular situations shall govern.

# Chapter 41

## Perpetuation of Proof for the Future

### Section 1

If there is a risk that proof concerning a circumstance of importance to a person's legal right may be lost, or difficult to obtain, and not action concerning the rights is pending, a lower court may take and perpetuate for the future proof in the form of witness testimony, expert opinions, views, or documentary evidence. However, proof may not be taken pursuant to this chapter for the purpose of investigating a crime.

### Section 2

Anyone desiring to take and perpetuate proof for the future shall apply to the court.

The application shall state that fact expected to be established by the proof, the nature of the proof, the grounds claimed by the applicant in support of the proposed proof-taking and, if possible, the other persons whose interests may be at stake.

### Section 3

The provisions on proof-taking outside a main hearing shall correspondingly apply to the perpetuation of proof for the future; if, however, in addition to the legal right of the applicant, the rights of another person can depend on the proof-taking, a notice to appear need not be given to such person absent special cause. No person is obliged to appear as a witness or an expert for the purpose of perpetuating proof in a court other than the one for the district in which he resides.

### Section 4

Costs occasioned by the taking and perpetuation of proof for the future shall be paid by the applicant.

If another person whose right may depend on the proof-taking was served with a notice to appear and thereafter attended the proof-taking, such person may be reimbursed by the applicant for necessary travel and maintenance expenses and for loss of time in an amount found reasonable by the court.

# Part Four

# Proceedings in the Lower Court

## I. Proceedings in Civil Cases

### Chapter 42

#### Summons and Preparatory Proceedings

**Section 1**

Anyone who desires the issuance of a summons shall file a written summons application with the court.

**Section 2**

In the summons application the plaintiff shall state:

1. the circumstances upon which he founds his action, presented in logical sequence and, whenever appropriate, in separate numbered paragraphs;

2. the demand for relief presented by the plaintiff;

3. the documentary evidence offered by the plaintiff;

4. the circumstances rendering the court competent, unless this is apparent from other allegations.

The application shall be signed by the plaintiff or his attorney in his own hand.

The plaintiff should annex to the application the originals or certified copies of the documentary evidence in his possession.

**Section 3**

If the summons application fails to comply with the regulations in section 2 or is otherwise incomplete, the court shall direct the plaintiff to cure the defect.

**Section 4**

If the plaintiff fails to obey a directive as under section 3, the application shall be dismissed if it is so incomplete that it cannot without essential inconvenience be used as basis for legal proceedings.

The application shall also be dismissed if it is manifest that the case cannot be entertained owing to a procedural hindrance. (SFS 1984:131)

**Section 5**

If the application is not dismissed, the court shall issue a summons calling upon the defendant to answer the claim. If the plaintiff's petition does not contain reasons for the claim as prescribed by law or if the claim otherwise is manifestly unfounded, however, the court may immediately pass judgment without issuing a summons.

If a summons is issued, it shall be served upon the defendant together with the summons application and the papers annexed thereto. (SFS 1984:131)

**Section 6**

Upon the issuance of the summons, preparation of the action shall commence.

During the preparation, the action shall be readied for trial so that the main hearing can be concluded in an uninterrupted sequence.

**Section 7**

At the outset of the preparation, the defendant shall immediately state his answer, which shall contain:

1. the procedural objections which the defendant wishes to urge;
2. a district statement of consent or opposition to the plaintiff's demand for relief;
3. if the plaintiff's demand for relief is opposed, the ground therefor including the defendant's position as to the basis of the plaintiff's claim, and a statement of the circumstances urged in defence; and
4. information as to the documentary evidence offered by the defendant.

The defendant should present immediately the originals or certified copies of the documentary evidence in his possession.

**Section 8**

During the preparation each party shall state the additional circumstances he wishes to allege and respond to his adversary's allegation. In addition, each party shall specify, to the extent not previously stated, the evidence upon which he desires to rely and what he intends to prove by each specified item. Documentary evidence not already presented shall be immediately submitted. Upon request of his adversary a party is obliged to indicate what other items of documentary evidence he has in his possession.

During the preparation the court shall attempt to ensure that the parties specify everything they wish to cite in the case and, by questions and reminders, shall attempt to remedy and unclear or incomplete statement.

The court may order separate preparation of separate issues or portions of the action. (SFS 1971:218)

**Section 8 a**

If the matter is such that a settlement out of court is permitted, a party may be directed finally to define his claim and state the evidence he invokes, if so required in view of the way in which the party has earlier conducted his case during the trial. After the time for making a statement has expired, the party may not invoke any new circumstance or any new evidence unless he renders it plausible that he has had a valid excuse for his failure earlier to invoke the circumstance or evidence. (SFS 1984:131)

**Section 9**

The preparation shall be oral. However, the court may order written preparation if a party's appearance would occasion unreasonable costs or extreme inconvenience, or if, in view of the nature of the action, written preparation is otherwise found more appropriate.

**Section 10**

With respect to oral preparation, the first preparatory session shall be scheduled to take place as soon as possible. The parties shall be called to attend the session, the plaintiff through a separate notice to appear and the defendant in the summons.

When the action is amenable to out of court settlement, each party shall be directed to appear with the consequence that otherwise a default judgment may be entered against him. If a party is to appear in person, the court shall direct him to do so on penalty of fine.

When the action is not such as is stated in the preceding paragraph, the plaintiff shall be directed to appear with the consequence that otherwise his claim in the action will be dismissed without prejudice to the commencement of a new proceeding. If he is to appear in person, the court shall direct him to do so on penalty of fine.

### Section 11

At oral preparation a party may not submit or read a written statement of his position or other written address. However, the summons application, or any other statement which may be made in writing pursuant to this Code, may be read; at the first preparatory session, the defendant, in response to the plaintiff's claim, may refer to a written answer submitted by him. If it is found that the allegations in the written answer do not constitute a complete response, the court shall attempt to remedy the defects by questioning the defendant.

### Section 12

If possible, the preparation shall be concluded at the first preparatory session. If this cannot be done, the case shall be scheduled for further preparation on a date fixed by the court. Proceedings in the case may not be postponed for a period longer than is unavoidably required.

The parties shall be notified to appear at a further preparatory session either orally at the preceding session or through special written notice. As to directions for the parties, the provisions in section 10, second and third paragraphs, shall apply; however, if it is found that the presence of one of the parties is not necessary, that party may be notified by a directive that does not call for the imposition of a sanction for non-appearance.

The court may direct continuation of the preparation through an exchange of writings.

### Section 13

The court may schedule a special hearing for the disposition of a procedural issue, or of a portion of the disputed matter that may be tried separately. As to such a hearing, the provisions in sections 10 and 12 shall correspondingly apply; however, if the hearing concerns the disposition of a procedural issue, in lieu of the directions stated in those sections, the parties shall be directed to appear on penalty of fine.

### Section 14

If written preparation is ordered, the defendant shall be directed in the summons to file a written answer with the court. When an answer is filed, the answer with the papers annexed thereto shall be served upon the plaintiff. If the court finds that a further exchange of writings is necessary, it may so direct.

If the defendant fails to submit an answer, the court shall immediately notify the parties to appear at an oral preparatory session. In other situations as well, the court may direct continuation of the preparation through oral proceedings.

**Section 15**

The court may issue detailed regulations as to the exchange of writings, between the parties and, in that connection, it may specify the issues upon which the parties shall express themselves.

**Section 16**

During the preparation, an order dismissing the action without reaching the merits may be issued.

**Section 17**

In an action amenable to out of court settlement, if it appears appropriate, the court should attempt to conciliate the parties during the preparation. If special mediation appears warranted, the court may direct the parties to appear at a conciliation session before a mediator appointed by the court.

**Section 18**

During the preparation, a default judgment and, in an action amenable to out of court settlement, a judgment based upon a party's consent to or renunciation of a claim, may be entered. A settlement agreement may also be confirmed by the court.

**Section 19**

For the purpose of assuring that all of the evidence will be available for presentation at the main hearing in an uninterrupted sequence, orders shall be issued during the preparation for obtaining expert opinions, documentary production, or objects for view or inspection, or for taking any other preparatory measure.

If evidence is to be taken outside the main hearing, orders thereon should also issue during the preparation.

If a party desires that a measure stated above be taken, he shall apply to the court therefor as soon as possible.

**Section 20**

As soon as the preparation has been concluded, the court shall fix a date for the main hearing, giving the parties, whenever possible, an opportunity to express themselves thereon. A main hearing may be scheduled for the disposition of a procedural issue or of a portion of the disputed matter that may be decided separately, although in other respects the action is not yet ready for trial.

The main hearing may be held in simplified form if no impediment of the kind referred to in chapter 43, section 2, exists and the parties also consent thereto. Such a main hearing may take place in immediate conjunction with the preparation or, provided that the same judge sits in the court, within fifteen days of completion of the preparatory hearing. Regardless of the consent of the parties a main hearing in simplified form may be held in immediate conjunction with the preparation if the appropriate resolution of the controversy appears plain to the court.

At a main hearing in simplified form all the attendant circumstances at the session when the preparatory hearing was concluded shall be considered to have occurred also at the main hearing without needing to be repeated at the latter. (SFS 1969:244)

### Section 21

The parties shall be notified to attend the main hearing either orally at the preceding court session or through separate written notice. As to the directions for the parties, the provisions in section 10, second and third paragraphs, and in section 13 shall apply.

As to notices to witnesses and experts to appear at the main hearing, the provisions in chapters 36 and 40 shall apply.

### Section 22

If a party desires to rely at the main hearing upon an item of evidence which he has not presented during the preparation, he shall immediately notify the court and his adversary thereof and indicate what he intends to prove by such item.

# Chapter 43

## Main Hearing

### Section 1

When the action is called, the court shall ascertain whether there is any impediment to an immediate full hearing and final disposition of the action.

### Section 2

The main hearing shall be cancelled and scheduled for a new date:

1. if a party who should be present in person has appeared only by his attorney;

2. if a witness or an expert who should be examined fails to appear;

3. if a party desires to allege a new, important ground or to present new evidence, and it is found that a postphonement is required in order to provide the adverse party with a reasonable opportunity to meet the new ground or evidence;

4. if there is otherwise an impediment to immediate trial and final disposition of the action.

If it can be assumed that the impediment will be removed prior to the conclusion of the session, the main hearing may be held.

**Section 3**

Although there is an impediment of the kind referred to in section 2, the main hearing may be commenced if it can be assumed that, pursuant to section 11, second paragraph, the hearing would be subject to continuance at a later session without a new main hearing and, further, that segmentation of the hearing would not adversely affect inquiry into the merits.

Even if the main hearing is cancelled, the court may hear the testimony of the party, witness, or expert who is present if it can be assumed that he will be unable to appear at a later session without unreasonable cost or extraordinary inconvenience. If it is of extraordinary importance for the investigation that other evidence be taken, or any other proceeding occur in conjunction with such testimony, this may be done. As to evidence thus taken, the provisions concerning proof-taking outside the main hearing shall apply to the extent relevant.

**Section 4**

The court is responsible for the orderly and systematic progress of the proceeding and may direct that separate issues or portions of the action be taken up individually. The court must also make certain that the action is fully developed and that irrelevant matters are not presented. Through questions and reminders, the court shall attempt to remedy any unclear or incomplete statement made in the course of the proceeding.

**Section 5**

The hearing shall be oral. The parties may not submit or read any written statement of position or other written address; however, the demand for relief may be read from a paper.

**Section 6**

A party shall truthfully account for his allegations in the action, respond to the allegations of his adversary, and answer questions put to him.

If a party makes a statement which is inconsistent with an assertion previously made by him, or if an inconsistency otherwise appears in his statements, he shall be asked to render an explanation thereon.

**Section 7**

At the hearing the plaintiff shall state his demand for relief and the defendant shall indicate whether he consents to, or opposes, the demand. Further, the parties, each in turn, shall present their allegations and respond to the allegations of the adverse party.

If the circumstances so warrant, at the outset of the hearing the court may summarize the issues in dispute.

A party's statements during the preparation may not be read unless his oral testimony at the hearing differs from his previous statement, or he fails to express himself on a matter covered by him at the preparation, or special cause otherwise justifies such reading.

When the hearing is held despite the absence of one of the parties, to the extent necessary, the absentee's position shall be presented by the court from the documents.

**Section 8**

After the parties have presented their allegations, the evidence shall be presented.

If a party is to testify under truth affirmation, unless special circumstances indicate otherwise, the party should be heard prior to the taking of witness testimony concerning the circumstance as to which the party shall be examined.

**Section 9**

After the evidence has been presented, the parties may state what they regard as necessary for the summation of their positions.

**Section 10**

If a party amends a statement previously made by him in the action, or adds something thereto, or claims a circumstance or evidence which was not mentioned prior to the commencement of the main hearing, the matter thus presented by the party may be disregarded if it can be assumed that the party's conduct was designed to delay the proceeding, to surprise his adversary, or to accomplish some other improper purpose.

**Section 11**

Apart from recesses authorized in chapter 1, section 9, the main hearing shall as far as possible continue without interruption until the action is ready for final disposition by the court. A main hearing once commenced may not be adjourned unless it was held pursuant to section 3, first paragraph, or a new important ground is interposed or knowledge of a new significant item of evidence is obtained subsequent to the commencement of the hearing, or the court otherwise deems adjournment unavoidably required. When the main hearing is adjourned, it shall be resumed as soon as can appropriately be done.

If the action is resumed after one or more adjournments and the total adjournment time does not exceed fifteen days, the main hearing may be continued. Otherwise a new main hearing shall be held; in an action of such an extent that the main hearing is expected to take at least four weeks, however, the court, considering the nature of the inquiry or any other special circumstance, may continue the main hearing rather than begin anew if it finds extraordinary cause for such continuance. If a main hearing held in simplified form is adjourned, a new main hearing shall be held without application of chapter 42, section 20, second paragraph.

The parties shall be notified to attend a postponed main hearing orally at the preceding session or by special written notice. As to the directions for parties, the provisions in chapter 42, section 10, second and third paragraphs, and section 13, shall apply; if an action is scheduled for a continued main hearing, in lieu of a direction pursuant to section 10, second paragraph, a party may be directed to appear with the consequence that otherwise either a default judgment may be entered against him or the action may be adjudicated notwithstanding his absence. (SFS 1969:244)

**Section 12**

When an action is scheduled for a continued or new main hearing, in order to make it possible to bring the action to a conclusion at that hearing, the court may direct resumption of the preparation and issue instructions necessary therefor.

**Section 13**

At a continued main hearing the action shall proceed from the stage it had reached at the conclusion of the previous hearing.

At a new main hearing the trial shall be commenced de novo. If an item of evidence was taken at an earlier hearing, the item shall be re-taken, provided that such re-taking is found to be of importance in the action, and that no impediment thereto exists. When an item of evidence is not re-taken, it shall be brought forward from the protocol and other documents concerning the earlier proof-taking.

## Chapter 44

### Consequences of Party Absence

#### Section 1

If both parties fail to appear at a hearing for oral preparation, the case shall be written off.

#### Section 2

In an action amenable to out of court settlement, if a party fails to appear at a hearing for oral preparation, and he was directed to appear with the consequence that otherwise a default judgment might be entered against him, on request of the appearing party, such a judgment shall be entered. If a default judgment is not requested, the case shall be written off.

However, if the non-appearing party is the defendant, on the request of the plaintiff, the action may be continued for oral preparation on a subsequent date. If the defendant fails to appear at the subsequent hearing, the rules in the first paragraph shall apply.

#### Section 3

In an action not amenable to out of court settlement, if the plaintiff fails to appear at a hearing for oral preparation, and he was directed to appear with the consequence that otherwise his claim would be dismissed without prejudice, the case shall be written off.

If the defendant fails to appear, and he was directed to appear on penalty of fine, in lieu of directing him to appear under the sanction of a new conditional fine, the court may order that he be brought before it in custody either immediately or on the date to which the session has been adjourned.

#### Section 4

As to the parties' non-appearance at main hearing sessions, the provisions in section 1, section 2, first paragraph, and section 3, shall apply.

When a party has been directed to appear with the consequence that otherwise either a default judgment may be entered against him or the action adjudicated notwithstanding his non-appearance, and no default judgment is entered, the court, on request of the appearing party, may try the action on the merits. When such a request is not presented, the case shall be written off.

### Section 5

In an action not amenable to out of court settlement, if a party directed to attend in person on penalty of fine appears by attorney only, the court, in lieu of directing him to appear under the sanction of a new conditional fine, may order that he be brought before it in custody either immediately or on the date to which the session has been adjourned.

### Section 6

If a party has been directed to appear on penalty of fine, or if he is to be brought before the court in custody and it is found that the order for bringing him to court cannot be executed, the preparation may nonetheless be concluded, or the action adjudicated on the merits notwithstanding the fact that the party has appeared by attorney only, or has failed to appear.

### Section 7

If one or both of the parties fails to appear at a special hearing for the disposition of a procedural issue, the issue may nonetheless be considered and determined.

### Section 8

When a judgment by default is entered against the plaintiff, his claim shall be dismissed on the merits unless the claim has been consented to by the defendant, or it is otherwise plain that the claim is well-founded.

A judgment by default against the defendant shall be based upon the plaintiff's allegations of the circumstances in the action to the extent that the defendant has received notice of the allegations and that they are not contrary to matters that are generally known. To the extent that the allegations are insufficient to entitle the plaintiff to requested relief, or that the claim is otherwise plainly ill-founded, the claim shall be dismissed.

A judgment by default shall be marked as such.

### Section 9

A party, against whom a judgment by default has been entered, may apply for reopening of the case at the court in which the action was instituted within one month of the date on which the judgment was served upon him. If reopening is not applied for, the judgment becomes immune to attack to the extent that it is against the party in default.

An application for reopening shall be submitted in writing. If the default judgment was entered during the preparation, the application should contain everything necessary to complete the preparation by the applicant.

#### Section 10

When an application for reopening is accepted, the action, to the extent reopening has been applied for, shall be resumed at the stage it had reached prior to the hearing at which the party failed to appear.

If the party again fails to appear, and a default judgment is entered against him, his right to a reopening is forfeited.

# II Proceedings in Criminal Cases

## Chapter 45

### Commencement of Public Prosecutions

#### Section 1

A prosecutor who desires to institute a public prosecution shall file with the court a written application for a summons against the person to be charged; however, to the extent found appropriate, the court may authorize the prosecutor to issue a summons.

A public prosecution is deemed commenced when the summons application is filed with the court or, if the prosecutor has issued the summons, when it is served upon the defendant.

If a person is undergoing prosecution for an offence, no new prosecution for that offence may be instituted against him.

#### Section 2

Prosecutions for procedural offences may be instituted without a summons.

If a person commits any other offence before the court at a session, prosecution for the offence may be instituted without a summons if the court, considering the nature of the offence and other circumstances, finds it appropriate.

Any legal prescription authorizing the institution of a public prosecution without a summons in specified cases shall govern.

**Section 3**

If prosecutions have been instituted either against one person for multiple offences or against several persons alleged to have participated in the same offence, the prosecutions shall be consolidated, unless the court finds separate proceedings more suitable. Prosecutions instituted against several persons for different offences may be jointly processed if it is of advantage for the inquiry that is to be made at trial.

Prosecutions may not be joined unless they have been properly instituted at the same court and the same rules of procedure apply to each.

For cause, prosecutions consolidated for trial may again be separated. (SFS 1956:587)

**Section 4**

In the summons application the prosecutor shall identify:

1. the defendant;

2. the injured person, if any;

3. the criminal act charged, specifying the time and place of its commission and the other particulars required for its identification and the applicable statutory section or sections;

4. the evidence he desires to offer and what he intends to prove by each specified item; and

5. the circumstances rendering the court competent, unless this is apparent from other allegations.

If the prosecutor, pursuant to chapter 22, section 2, desires to initiate simultaneously with the prosecution a private claim, he shall state in the application the claim, the circumstances upon which it is founded, the evidence he desires to offer, and what he intends to prove by each specified item.

If the defendant is or has been under arrest or in detention, or in confinement on suspicion of the offence prosecuted, information to this effect shall be stated in the summons application. A note of the date of deprivation of liberty shall also be given.

The application shall be signed by the prosecutor. (SFS 1973:45)

**Section 5**

A prosecution, once instituted, may not be amended. However, the prosecutor may extend the prosecution against the same defendant to encompass another criminal act if the court, considering the investigation and other circumstances, finds it appropriate.

After the commencement of a prosecution the prosecutor or the injured person may initiate without a summons a private claim based on the offence if the court, considering the inquiry to be made at trial and other circumstances, finds it appropriate. The same applies when the claim has been taken over by a third party.

It is not deemed an amendment of the prosecution if, with respect to the same criminal act, the prosecutor narrows his charge, asserts a statutory provision other than the one stated in the summons or alleges a new circumstance in support of the prosecution. (SFS 1969:588)

### Section 6

When the prosecutor desires to commence a prosecution for an offence in accordance with section 2, first or second paragraph, or to extend the prosecution under section 5, or when he, the injured person, or anyone who has taken over the injured person's claim under the aforesaid section desires to institute a private claim based upon the offence, it may be done either orally before the court or in writing. The defendant shall be notified of the charge of claim. Such prosecution is deemed commenced when presented to the court. (SFS 1969:588)

### Section 7

If a preliminary investigation was held in the case, when the prosecution is instituted, or as soon as possible thereafter, the prosecutor shall submit to the court a copy of the record or notes of the investigation, as well as the documents and objects which the prosecutor intends to offer as evidence.

### Section 8

The summons application shall be dismissed if the court finds it plain that the person initiating the prosecution is not authorized to prosecute for the offence, or that the action, by reason of any other procedural hindrance, cannot be heard and determined upon the merits.

### Section 9

If the application is not dismissed, the court shall issue a summons calling upon the defendant to answer the charge.

The summons together with the summons application and the papers annexed thereto shall be served upon the defendant.

**Section 10**

In the summons the court shall also direct the defendant to state to the court, either orally or in writing, the evidence he desires to offer at the main hearing and to indicate what he intends to prove by each specified item. This does not apply, however, if it can be assumed from the confession of the defendant or other circumstance that no statement of evidence is required. The prosecutor shall be notified by the court of any statement so submitted. (SFS 1976:1137)

**Section 11**

For the purpose of making possible full trial of the action at the main hearing in an uninterrupted sequence, the court may direct the prosecutor to complete the preliminary investigation or, if no investigation has been held, to conduct one.

**Section 12**

For the purpose of assuring that all of the evidence will be available for presentation at the main hearing in an uninterrupted sequence, orders shall be issued without delay for obtaining expert opinions, documentary production, or objects for view or inspection, or for taking any other preparatory measure.

If evidence is to be taken outside the main hearing, orders thereon shall be issued without delay.

If a party desires that a measure stated above be taken, he shall apply to the court therefor as soon as possible.

**Section 13**

If it is found that, for disposition of an issue of the kind referred to in section 11 or 12, a party or a third person should be examined, the court shall issue orders thereon in the manner it deems appropriate. As to the attendance of an arrested or detained defendant, the court shall issue the appropriate directive to provide for his presence.

**Section 14**

As soon as possible, the court shall fix a date for the main hearing. A main hearing may be scheduled for the disposition of a procedural issue, or of a portion of the action that may be decided separately, although in other respects the action is not ready for trial.

If the defendant is under arrest or in detention, the main hearing shall be held within one week of the date of the commencement of the prosecution unless, as a result of a measure stated in section 11 or 12 or any other circumstance, a longer postponement is necessary. If the defendant is detained after the institution of prosecution, the time within which the main hearing is to be held shall be computed from the date of his detention.

If a travel prohibition order has been issued to the defendant, the main hearing shall be held within one month of the date of the commencement of the prosecution unless, as a result of a measure stated in section 11 or 12 or any other circumstance, a longer postponement is necessary. If the travel prohibition has been ordered after the institution of prosecution, the time within which the main hearing is to be held shall be computed from the date of service of the order. (SFS 1981:1294)

**Section 15**

The prosecutor shall be given notice to appear at the main hearing. The injured person shall also be given notice to appear if he supports or joins in the prosecution, or if he is to be examined as part of the prosecutor's case. If the injured person is to appear in person, the court shall direct him to do so on penalty of fine.

The defendant shall be given notice to appear at the main hearing in the summons or through a separate notice. If he is required to appear in person or otherwise to be present, the direction shall be issued on penalty of fine. If there is cause to believe that the defendant would not obey such a direction, the court may order that he be brought to the main hearing in custody. If, pursuant to chapter 46, section 15, the action may be tried on the merits notwithstanding the fact that the defendant has appeared only by attorney or has failed to appear, he shall be reminded thereof in the notice. The court shall issue the appropriate directive to provide for the presence of an arrested or detained defendant.

As to the notices to witnesses and experts to appear as the main hearing, the provisions in chapters 36 and 40 shall apply. (SFS 1982:283)

**Section 16**

Summonses issued by the prosecutor shall have the content stated in section 4 concerning summons application and shall be signed by the prosecutor.

In the summons the prosecutor shall also direct the defendant, within a specified time fixed by the prosecutor, to state to the court, either orally or in writing, the evidence he desires to offer at the main hearing and what he wishes to prove with each particular item. This does not apply, however, if, owing to the confession of the defendant or to any other circumstance, the prosecutor finds it plain that no evidence will be offered by the defendant. If appropriate, the prosecutor may in the summons notify the defendant to appear at the main hearing.

When a prosecutor schedules an action for main hearing, he shall observe the regulations concerning the time for main hearings issued by the court; the prosecutor may also issue the notices to appear and directions referred to in section 15.

The summons together with the documents annexed thereto shall be served upon the defendant. Immediately after service the summons and proof of its service shall be submitted to the court. (SFS 1976:1137)

### Section 17

If a party desires to rely at the main hearing upon an item of evidence that he did not refer to earlier; he shall immediately notify the court and his adversary of the item and indicate what he intends to prove by it.

### Section 18

Repealed by SFS 1976:567.

## Chapter 46

### Main Hearing in Cases with Public Prosecution

### Section 1

When the action is called, the court shall ascertain whether there is any impediment to an immediate full hearing and final disposition of the action.

### Section 2

The main hearing shall be cancelled and scheduled for a new date:

1. if the prosecutor is not present;

2. if the defendant fails to appear either in person or by attorney or, if directed to attend in person, appears only by attorney, and the situation is not such that the case may be tried despite his absence;

3. if, pursuant to statutory prescription, the defendant must have a defence counsel, and such counsel is not present or immediately appointed;

4. if an injured person, a witness or an expert who should be examined fails to appear;

5. if a party desires to allege a new, important ground or to present new evidence, and it is found that a postponement is required in order to provide the adverse party with a reasonable opportunity to meet the new ground or evidence; or

6. if there is otherwise an impediment to immediate trial and final disposition of the action.

If it can be assumed that the impediment will be removed prior to the conclusion of the session, the main hearing may be held.

**Section 3**

Although there is an impediment of the kind referred to in section 2, first paragraph, 4–6, the main hearing may be commenced if it can be assumed that pursuant to section 11, second paragraph, the hearing would be subject to continuance at a later session without a new main hearing and, further, that segmentation of the hearing would not adversely affect the inquiry on the merits.

Even if the main hearing is cancelled, the court may hear the testimony of an injured person, witness, or expert who is present if it can be assumed that he will be unable to appear at a later session without unreasonable cost or extraordinary inconvenience. If it is of extraordinary importance for the inquiry that other evidence be taken or any other proceeding occur in conjunction with such testimony, this may be done. As to evidence thus taken, the provisions concerning proof-taking outside the main hearing shall apply to the extent relevant.

**Section 4**

The court is responsible for the orderly and systematic progress of the proceeding and may direct that separate issues or portions of the action be taken up individually. The court must also make certain that the action is fully developed and that irrelevant matters are not presented. Through questions and reminders, the court shall attempt to remedy any unclear or incomplete statement made in the course of the proceeding.

**Section 5**

The hearing shall be oral. The parties may not submit or read any written statement of position or other written address; however, the charge may be read from a paper.

**Section 6**

At the hearing the prosecutor shall state his charge and the defendant shall be requested to indicate whether he admits or denies the charged criminal act.

Thereafter the prosecutor shall introduce his case and set forth the particulars upon which it is based. Following the prosecutor's opening, the injured person shall be examined.

The defendant shall be requested to state his case in an uninterrupted sequence and, in conjunction therewith, to respond to the allegations of the prosecutor or of the injured person. With the consent of the court, the prosecutor and the injured person may put questions to the defendant. Thereafter questions may be put by the defence counsel.

During the examination of the injured person, or of the defendant, no written rendition of a statement previously made by him before the court or before a prosecutor or a police authority may be read unless his oral testimony at the hearing differs from his previous statement or he fails to express himself at the examination.

When a main hearing is held despite the absence of the injured party, or the defendant, to the extent necessary the absentee's position shall be presented by the court from the documents.

**Section 7**

If there is cause to believe that a party in the presence of another party, through fear or otherwise, is likely to be inhibited from telling the truth unreservedly, or if a party hinders another party from testifying by interrupting or otherwise, the court may exclude the party from the courtroom during the examination; this prescription as to parties shall also apply to an injured person who presents no claim on his own behalf in the proceeding.

Upon the return of the person excluded during the examination, he shall be informed as to what occurred in his absence.

**Section 8**

After the injured party and the defendant have been examined, the evidence shall be presented.

**Section 9**

If the offence is such that a sanction other than a fine can be expected, or if special cause otherwise warrants it, a presentation shall be made concerning the punishments to which the defendant has previously been sentenced and regarding his standard of living and the individual circumstances which can be assumed to be of importance.

**Section 10**

After the evidence has been presented, the parties may state what they regard as necessary for the summation of their positions.

### Section 11

Apart from recesses authorized in chapter 1, section 9, the main hearing shall as far as possible continue without interruption until the action is ready for final disposition by the court. A main hearing once commenced may not be adjourned unless it was held pursuant to section 3, first paragraph, or a new important ground is interposed or knowledge of a new significant item of evidence is obtained subsequent to the commencement of the hearing, or the court otherwise deems adjournment unavoidably required. When the main hearing is adjourned, it shall be resumed as soon as can appropriately be done. When the defendant is in detention, the hearing shall be resumed within a week of the day on which the prior session terminated or, if he was detained after the termination of that session, within a week of the day on which his detention commenced, unless, owing to special circumstances, a longer adjournment is required.

If the case is resumed after one or more adjournments and the total adjournment time does not exceed fifteen days, the main hearing may be continued. Otherwise a new main hearing shall be held; in an action of such an extent that the main hearing is expected to take at least four weeks, however, the court, considering the nature of the inquiry or any other special circumstance, may continue the main hearing rather than begin anew if it finds extraordinary cause for such continuance.

The parties shall be notified to attend a postponed main hearing orally at the preceding session or by special written notice. As to directions concerning appearances, the provisions in chapter 45, section 15, shall apply. (SFS 1969:244)

### Section 12

When an action is scheduled for a continued or a new main hearing, in order to make it possible to bring the action to a conclusion at that hearing, the court may direct the measures deemed suitable. As to such measures, the provisions in chapter 45, section 11 to 13, shall govern.

### Section 13

At a continued main hearing the case shall proceed from the stage it had reached at the conclusion of the previous hearing.

At a new main hearing the trial shall be commenced de novo. If an item of evidence was taken at an earlier hearing, the item shall be re-taken, provided that such re-taking is found to be of importance in the action, and that no impediment thereto exists. When the item of evidence is not re-taken, it shall be brought forward from the protocol and other documents concerning the earlier proof-taking.

**Section 14**

If an injured person who is to be examined as part of the prosecutor's case fails to appear in person at a main hearing, in lieu of directing a new conditional fine, the court may order that he be brought before it in custody either immediately or on the date to which the session has been adjourned.

**Section 15**

If the defendant fails to appear at a main hearing, or, if he appears by attorney only although directed to attend in person, the court shall either direct a new conditional fine or order that he be brought before it in custody either immediately or on the date to which the session has been adjourned.

If the matter can be investigated satisfactorily, the action may be tried on the merits notwithstanding the fact that the defendant has appeared only by attorney or has failed to appear, if

1. there is no cause to impose a criminal sanction other than fine, imprisonment for at most three months, a conditional sentence or probation, or a combination of such sanctions, or

2. the defendant, after service of the summons upon him, has fled or remains concealed in such a way that he cannot be brought to the main hearing.

In a case as referred to in the second paragraph (1) the defendant may be sentenced to imprisonment only if he previously has failed to appear in person at a main hearing or if he appeared by attorney only although directed to attend in person. If, after the earlier session, the prosecution has been extended to comprise an additional offence, a sentence of imprisonment may be imposed only if there was cause to sentence to imprisonment for the offences to which the prosecution related before it was extended.

As equivalent to the sanctions stated in the second paragraph (1) shall be treated an order pursuant to chapter 34, section 1, first paragraph, of the Penal Code. This shall not apply, however, if, in conjunction with the order, parole from imprisonment is to be declared to have been forfeited in respect of a term of imprisonment exceeding three months.

A case as referred to in the second paragraph (2) may be adjudicated even if notice of the hearing has not been served upon the defendant.

Procedural issues may be decided despite non-appearance of the defendant. (SFS 1982:283)

### Section 16

If a defence counsel is not present when the law requires that the defendant shall have one, if possible, the court shall appoint a person present in the court and authorized to accept such a commission.

## Chapter 47

### Commencement of Private Prosecutions and Main Hearing with Private Complaints

### Section 1

An injured person who desires to institute a prosecution shall file with the court a written application for a summons against the person to be charged. The prosecution shall be deemed commenced when the summons application is filed with the court.

If the defendant desires to initiate in the pending case a criminal action against the injured person or the prosecutor for malicious or unjustified prosecution, false accusation, or any other false charge concerning a crime, he may do so without a summons either orally before the court or in writing. Anyone against whom a criminal action is thus commenced shall be given notice of it. (SFS 1948:453)

### Section 2

In the summons application the injured person shall identify:

1. the defendant;

2. the criminal act charged, specifying the time and place of its commission, the other particulars required for its identification, and the applicable statutory section or sections;

3. the private claim which the injured person desires to assert, and the circumstances upon which the claim is founded;

4. the documentary evidence offered by the injured person; and

5. the circumstances, rendering the court competent, unless this is apparent from other allegations.

The application shall be signed by the injured person or his attorney in his own hand.

If the offence is such that the injured person is not entitled to initiate a prosecution unless the prosecutor has decided not to prosecute, a certification that such a decision was issued shall be annexed to the application. The injured person should also annex to the application the originals or certified copies of the documentary evidence in his possession.

**Section 3**

If the summons application fails to comply with the regulations in section 2 or is otherwise incomplete, or if the certification referred to in section 2, third paragraph, is not produced, the court shall direct the injured person to cure the defect.

**Section 4**

If the plaintiff fails to obey a directive as under section 3, the application shall be dismissed if it is so incomplete that it cannot without essential inconvenience be uses as basis for legal proceedings in the question of liability. The same applies if a certification referred to in section 2, third paragraph, has not been furnished. (SFS 1984:131)

**Section 5**

If the application is not dismissed, the court shall issue a summons calling upon the defendant to answer the claim. If the plaintiff's petition does not contain reasons for the claim as prescribed by law or if the claim otherwise is manifestly ungrounded, however, the court may immediately pass judgment without issuing a summons.

If a summons is issued, it shall be served upon the defendant together with the summons application and the papers annexed thereto. (SFS 1984:131)

**Section 6**

Upon the issuance of the summons, preparation of the action shall commence.

During the preparation, the action shall be readied for trial so that the main hearing can be concluded in an uninterrupted sequence.

**Section 7**

During the preparation, the defendant should state whether he admits or denies the criminal act and present his position as to the circumstances on which the prosecution is based; he should also state the circumstances which he desires to rely upon. Thereafter each party in turn should state the additional circumstances he desires to claim and respond to the circumstances alleged by his adversary. In addition, each party should specify, to the extent not previously stated, the evidence upon which he desires to rely and indicate what he intends to prove by each specified item. Any document not already presented shall be submitted immediately.

The court may order separate preparation of separate issues or portions of the action.

**Section 8**

The preparation shall be oral. However, the court may order written preparation if a party's appearance would occasion unreasonable costs or extreme inconvenience or if, in view of the nature of the action, written preparation is otherwise found more appropriate.

**Section 9**

With respect to oral preparation, the first preparatory session shall be scheduled to take place as soon as possible. If the defendant is in detention, the first preparatory session shall be held within one week of the date of his detention unless, owing to special circumstances, a longer postponement is necessary. If a travel prohibition order has been issued to the defendant, the first preparatory session shall be held within one month of the date of service of the order. The parties shall be notified to attend the first preparatory session, the injured person through a separate notice to appear and the defendant in the summons.

The injured person shall be directed to appear with the consequence that otherwise he forfeits his right to prosecute the offence. If the injured person is to appear in person, the court shall direct him to do so on penalty of fine.

The defendant shall be directed to appear on penalty of fine. As to the appearance of a defendant who is in detention, the court shall issue the appropriate directive to provide for his presence. (SFS 1981:1294)

**Section 10**

At oral preparation a party may not submit or read a written statement of his position or other written address. However, the summons application or any other statement which may be made in writing pursuant to this Code may be read; at the first preparatory session the defendant, in response to the charge, may refer to a written answer submitted by him. If it is found that the allegations in the written answer do not constitute a complete response, the court shall attempt to remedy the defects by questioning the defendant.

**Section 11**

If possible, the preparation shall be concluded at the first preparatory session. If this cannot be done, the case shall be scheduled for further preparation on a date fixed by the court. Proceedings in the case may not be postponed for a period longer than is unavoidably required. If the defendant is in detention, the session for continued preparation shall be held within one week of the day on which the previous hearing terminated or, if the defendant was placed in detention after that hearing, within one week of the day of his detention, unless, owing to special circumstances, a longer adjournment is required. The parties shall be notified to appear at a further preparatory session either orally at the preceding session or through special written notice.

As to directions for the parties, the provisions in section 9, second and third paragraphs, shall apply; however, if it is found that the presence of one of the parties is not necessary, that party may be notified by a directive that does not call for the imposition of a sanction for non-appearance.

The court may direct continuation of the preparation through an exchange of writings.

**Section 12**

The court may schedule a special hearing for the disposition of a procedural issue or of a portion of the case that may be tried separately. As to such a hearing, the provisions in sections 9 and 11 shall correspondingly apply, however, if the hearing concerns the disposition of a procedural issue, in lieu of the directions stated in those sections, the injured person shall be directed to appear on penalty of fine.

**Section 13**

If both parties fail to appear at a hearing for oral preparation, the case shall be written off.

**Section 14**

If the injured party fails to appear at a hearing for oral preparation, and he was directed to appear on pain of forfeiture of his right to prosecute for the offence, on request of the defendant, a declaration of such forfeiture shall be pronounced; when a declaration is not requested, the case shall be written off.

If the defendant fails to appear, and he was directed to appear on penalty of fine, in lieu of directing him to appear under the sanction of a new conditional fine, the court may order that he be brought before it in custody either immediately or on the date to which the session has been adjourned.

**Section 15**

If the injured person or the defendant appears by attorney although directed to attend in person on penalty of fine, in lieu of directing him to appear under the sanction of a new conditional fine, the court may order that he be brought before it in custody either immediately or on the date to which the session has been adjourned.

### Section 16

If a party has been directed to appear on penalty of fine, or if he is to be brought before the court in custody, but it is found that the order for bringing him to court cannot be executed, the preparation may nonetheless be concluded notwithstanding the fact that the party has appeared only by attorney or has failed to appear.

### Section 17

During the preparation, if one or both of the parties fails to appear at a special hearing for the disposition of a procedural issue, the issue may nonetheless be considered and determined.

### Section 18

When the court, pursuant to section 14, has declared that the injured person has forfeited his right to prosecute for the offence, the injured person may apply to the court for reinstatement of the case.

The application for reinstatement shall be submitted in writing within one month of the date on which the order was pronounced. If the injured person again fails to appear, his right to reinstatement of the case shall be forfeited.

### Section 19

If written preparation is ordered, the defendant shall be directed in the summons to file a written answer with the court. When an answer is filed, the answer with the papers annexed thereto shall be served upon the injured person. If the court finds that a further exchange of writings is necessary, it may so direct.

If the defendant fails to submit an answer, the court shall immediately notify the parties to appear at an oral preparatory session. In other situations as well, the court may direct continuation of the preparation through oral proceeding.

### Section 20

The court may issue detailed regulations as to the exchange of writings between the parties and, in that connection, it may specify the issues upon which the parties shall express themselves.

### Section 21

During the preparation, an order dismissing the action without reaching the merits may be issued.

**Section 22**

As soon as the preparation has been concluded, the court shall fix a date for the main hearing, giving the parties, whenever possible, an opportunity to express themselves thereon. A main hearing may be scheduled for the disposition of a procedural issue or of a portion of the action that may be decided separately although in other respects the action is not ready for trial.

If the defendant is in detention, the main hearing shall be held within one week of the day on which the preparation was concluded or, if he was detained after conclusion of preparation, within one week of the day of his detention.

If a travel prohibition order has been issued to the defendant, the main hearing shall be held within one month of the day on which the preparation was concluded. If issued thereafter, the time shall be computed from the date of service of the order. (SFS 1981:1294)

**Section 23**

The parties shall be notified to attend the main hearing either orally at the preceding court session or through separate written notice.

As to directions for the parties, the provisions in section 9, second and third paragraphs, and section 12 shall apply. If there is cause to believe that the defendant would not obey such a direction, the court may order that he be brought before it in custody. As to the attendance of a defendant who is in detention, the court shall issue the appropriate directive to provide for his presence.

As to notices to witnesses and experts to appear at the main hearing, the provisions in chapters 36 and 40 shall apply.

**Section 24**

As to private prosecutions in other respects, the provisions in chapter 45, section 1, third paragraph, and sections 2, 3, 5, 6, 8, 12 and 17, shall correspondingly apply.

Concerning main hearings in private prosecutions, the provisions in chapter 46 shall correspondingly apply; however, in such cases, the following diverging rules shall govern:

1. As to notices to appear at adjourned main hearings, and directions for the parties, the provisions in section 23 of this chapter shall govern.

2. If both parties fail to appear at a main hearing, the case shall be written off. As to the consequences of the non-appearance of an injured person, his failure to attend in person, and the reinstatement of cases, the provisions in sections 14 to 16 and 18 shall correspondingly apply. If both parties, or one of them, fail to appear at a special

hearing for the disposition of a procedural issue, the issue may nonetheless be considered and determined.

3. When a case is fixed for a continued or a new main hearing, in lieu of a measure referred to in chapter 46, section 14, the court may order renewed preparation and issue regulations necessary for such additional preparation.

## Chapter 48

### Order of Summary Punishment by Fine and Summary Imposition of Breach-of-Regulations Fine

*General provisions*

#### Section 1

An issue of criminal liability subject to public prosecution may, under the conditions prescribed in this chapter, be brought up by a prosecutor by an order of summary punishment and by a policeman by an order of fine for breach of regulations. An order as aforesaid takes effect in lieu of prosecution to the extent stated in section 3.

Further regulations concerning the application of this chapter are issued by the Government or by an authority determined by the Government. (SFS 1974:573)

#### Section 2

An order as stated in this chapter implies submission to the suspect for his consent, immediately or within a specific time, of a directive to pay a fine fixed in the case of summary punishment, according to what the prosecutor considers warranted by the offence and, in the case of a fine for breach of regulations, as prescribed in section 14.

When the offence calls for forfeiture of property or any similar specially prescribed sanction, the sanction shall also be submitted to the suspect for approval. (SFS 1968:193)

#### Section 3

In an order as stated in this chapter has been issued for approval within a specific time, an issue of criminal liability for the offence may not be brought up anew until that time has expired.

An order consented to by the suspect shall have the same effect as a judgment which has become conclusive.

*Summary punishment by fine*

**Section 4**

An order of summary punishment by fine may be issued in respect of an offence punishable only by fine, but not by fines for which the law defines a special computation basis, and in respect of an offence punishable by day-fine or by imprisonment for at most six months. If the offence is punishable by day-fine, however, an order of summary punishment may be issued only when a single or multiple offence as aforesaid is deemed to warrant at most one hundred day-fines. (SFS 1982:1123)

**Section 5**

An order of summary punishment by fine may not be issued,

unless prerequisites for public prosecution exist,

unless the order includes all justiciable offences committed by the suspect to the prosecutor's knowledge,

if the injured party has declared that he intends to institute a civil claim in consequence of the offence or has requested institution of prosecution.

Special provisions exist governing the conditions for use of orders of summary punishment by fine in military criminal cases. (SFS 1975:670)

**Section 6**

Orders of summary punishment by fine shall be made in writing and signed by the prosecutor.

In the order the prosecutor shall identify

1. the suspect,

2. the criminal act, specifying the time and place of its commission and other particulars required for its identification,

3. the statutory section or sections applicable,

4. the punishment by fine and the specially prescribed sanctions submitted to the suspect for consent. (SFS 1968:193)

**Section 7**

If an order of summary punishment by fine is issued for consent within a specific time, the suspect shall, by an entry in the order or otherwise,

be notified of the manner for consent and of the time specified therefor, be notified that, if the order is not consented to, prosecution may take place after the expiration of the specified time. (SFS 1968:193)

### Section 8

An order of summary punishment by fine shall be delivered or despatched to the suspect.

The Government may direct that, in lieu of the order, a written notice may be delivered or despatched which records the content of the order and the notifications stated in section 7. (SFS 1974:573)

### Section 9

An order of summary punishment by fine is approved by the suspect signing and submitting to the proper recipient a declaration that the acknowledges the charge and accepts the punishment and the specially prescribed sanctions recorded in the order. Further regulations as to who shall receive such declaration are issued by the Government.

An approval signed on a document other than the order shall be valid only if it is clearly apparent which order it refers to. (SFS 1976:1137)

### Section 10

A written approval of an order of summary punishment by fine may be delivered by the suspect's attorney, instead of by himself personally, if a power of attorney in the original is submitted to the prosecutor containing, in addition to what is specified in chapter 12,

a declaration that the attorney is authorized to approve an order of summary punishment on the suspect's behalf,

a statement of the offence to which the approval shall relate, with indication of the nature of the offence and the time and place of its commission,

a statement of the maximal monetary sanction the suspect consents to,

a statement of the specially prescribed sanction in question and which the suspect consents to.

If such power of attorney has been submitted to the prosecutor, the attorney may accept documents in the matter on the suspect's behalf. (SFS 1976:1137)

### Section 11

If an order of summary punishment by fine concerns solely a fine, and the fine is to be paid to an authority determined by the Government without written consents having been given, the payment is regarded as consent unless it is apparent that the suspect did not intend to consent to the order. (SFS 1974:573)

**Section 12**

Consent to an order after the prosecutor has issued a summons or summons application is without effect. (SFS 1968:193)

**Section 12 a**

If the prosecutor finds that, owing to a writing error, faulty calculation or other similar oversight, an order of summary punishment to which consent has been given contains a manifest inaccuracy, he shall, after the person consenting thereto has been afforded the opportunity to make a statement, direct that the order be corrected.

Correction may not be made if the person consenting to the order objects thereto.

A correction may not entail raising of the penalty. (SFS 1982:1123)

*Fine for breach of regulations*

**Section 13**

An order of fine for breach of regulations may be issued in respect of an offence punishable only by fine immediately in money, but not fines for which the law defines a special computation basis, and for which fine for breach of regulations is imposed as prescribed in section 14.

The provisions concerning orders of fine for breach of regulations are not applicable if a special condition is prescribed for public prosecution. (SFS 1968:193)

**Section 14**

The Government may issue directions governing the maximum amount at which a fine for breach of regulations may be fixed and concerning other limitations on the use of orders of fine for breach of regulations.

The Chief State Prosecutor, in consultation with the National Police Board, decides on the offences for which fines for breach of regulations shall be imposed.

The Chief State Prosecutor determines for different offences the amounts to be imposed as fine for breach of regulations. He also indicates the basis for computing joint fines for several offences in this respect. For special cause the Chief State Prosecutor may direct a state prosecutor to determine the amount of fine for certain breaches of regulations. (SFS 1974:573)

**Section 15**

An order of fine for breach of regulations may not be issued,

if the suspect denies the charge,

unless the order includes all justiciable offences committed by the suspect to the policeman's knowledge,

if there is reason to suppose that an action for a private claim will be instituted, or

if there is reason to suppose that the offence should warrant disciplinary punishment of a member of the armed forces.

An order should not be issued if, in other cases, it may be deemed warranted that a prosecutor considers the desirability of summary punishment or prosecution for the offence. (SFS 1975:670)

**Section 16**

An order of fine for breach of regulations shall be made in writing and signed by the policeman.

The order should be issued in the presence of the suspect and the suspect shall be given the opportunity immediately to consent to the order.

If an order is issued in the absence of the suspect or if the suspect is present when the order is issued but needs time for consideration, the policeman may deliver the order to him for later decision as to consent. (SFS 1968:193)

**Section 17**

The provisions in section 6, second paragraph (1), (2) and (4), and in sections 7, 9, 11 and 12a apply also to an order of fine for breach of regulations. What is stated concerning a prosecutor in section 12a shall apply instead to a policeman. (SFS 1982:1123)

**Section 18**

If a policeman, in immediate conjunction with the issue and approval of an order of fine for breach of regulations, finds that the order contains a manifestly incorrect statement, and if this relates to a matter other than that the amount of the fine is too low, the policeman shall, if it can be done at once, notwithstanding section 3, second paragraph, authorize the suspect to strike out the approval. If he does so, the order shall be withdrawn. A new order may thereafter be issued. (SFS 1968:193)

**Section 19**

If an order of fine for breach of regulations is approved after the prosecutor has issued a summons or summons application, the approval is without effect. IF the approval takes place after an order of summary punishment has been issued, the approval is also without effect unless the prosecutor who issued the order of summary punishment declares the approval valid and withdraws the order of summary punishment. (SFS 1968:193)

**Section 20**

The Government may direct that an order of fine for breach of regulations may be issued also by a prosecutor or customs official. The provisions in this chapter applying to policemen apply correspondingly to those to whom such a direction refers. (SFS 1974:573)

# Part Five

# Proceedings in Courts of Appeals

## Chapter 49

### Appeals from Judgments and Orders of Lower Courts

#### Section 1

Appeal from a lower court judgment shall be sought by regular appeal.

A party against whom a default judgment was entered may not appeal from the judgment; his right to a reopening of the case following the entry of such a judgment is prescribed in chapter 44, section 9.

In an action amenable to out of court settlement, if a party has undertaken not to appeal from the judgment after the controversy arose, the undertaking shall be given effect; however, a commitment prior to the entry of judgment shall not be effective unless a reciprocal undertaking was made by the adverse party.

#### Section 2

Appeal from a lower court final order shall be sought by limited appeal. However, when an order dismissing a specified part of a case without reaching the merits is issued in conjunction with a judgment, review of the order shall be sought by regular appeal.

A party entitled to apply for reinstatement of a case terminated by a final order may not appeal from the order.

#### Section 3

If a lower court, in an order rendered in the course of the proceedings, has rejected an application for disqualification of a judge, or has overruled an objection based upon an alleged procedural hindrance, and the order is not one from which, pursuant to section 7, no appeal of any kind may be taken, a party desiring to appeal from the order must give a formal notice of exception immediately, if the order is pronounced at a hearing, and otherwise, within a week of service of the order upon him; if a party fails to take exception within the time prescribed, he forfeits his right to appellate review of the order. If a timely exception is taken, the court shall decide, with reference to the particular circumstances involved, whether an appeal shall be taken separately or only in conjunction with an appeal from the judgment or final order in the case. An appeal taken separately shall be brought by limited appeal.

**Section 4**

Appeals from the following lower court orders rendered in the course of the proceedings shall be brought separately:

1. orders dismissing an attorney, assistant or defence counsel;

2. orders denying a third persons's application for intervention in an action;

3. orders directing a party or a third person to produce documentary evidence or to make an object accessible for view or inspection, or if, pursuant to chapter 3, section 3, 5, or the Freedom of the Press Act, section 9, first paragraph, 5, or the Radio Responsibility Act (1966:756) or section 11, 5, of the Act Concerning Responsibility for Radio and Cassette Newspapers (1982:521), a court finds it to be of extreme importance that a statement referred to therein is made in the examination of a witness or of a party under truth affirmation;

4. orders concerning final imposition of a conditional fine, detention, liability for a procedural offence, or liability of a person other than a party or an intervenor to furnish compensation for costs occasioned in the proceedings;

5. orders concerning compensation or advance payment out of public funds to an injured person or concerning compensation or advance payment to an assistant, defence counsel, witness, expert or any person other than a party or intervenor;

6. orders in a civil case concerning provisional attachment or other measure as stated in chapter 15, and orders in a criminal case concerning detention or any measure stated in chapters 25–28;

7. orders denying an application for an assistant or defence counsel or appointing to such a commission a person other than the one proposed by the party;

8. orders on matters other than those referred to in 5 or 7 relating to public legal aid; or

9. orders denying an application for legal aid to a suspect in a criminal case or concerning compensation or advance payment to a party enjoying such privilege.

A separate appeal shall be brought by limited appeal. Any person desiring to appeal against an order referred to in 1, 2, 3, 7, 8 or 9 shall give formal notice of exception immediately, if the order was issued at a hearing, and otherwise within a week of service of the order upon him; in the event of failure to do so, he forfeits his right to appellate review of the order. The court shall determine immediately whether the exception was properly taken. (SFS 1981:510)

**Section 5**

If a lower court has issued an order concerning a matter enumerated in section 4 in conjunction with a judgment or final order, and the matter relates to an attorney, assistant defence counsel, witness, expert, or any person other than a party or intervenor, appeal from the order shall be brought by limited appeal. The same shall apply to an order of a lower court, issued in conjunction with a judgment or final order, concerning the liability of a public prosecutor to furnish compensation for litigation costs.

In other situations in which an order issued in conjunction with a judgment or final order concerns a matter enumerated in section 4, or relates to the liability of a party, an intervenor, or the treasury to furnish compensation for litigation costs, appeal from the order shall be brought in the same form as an appeal from the judgment or final order.

**Section 6**

Any party who is of the opinion that processing of the case has been delayed without cause by a lower court order may appeal from that order separately through limited appeal.

**Section 7**

A lower court order disqualifying a judge or granting an application for legal aid to a suspect in a criminal case is not subject to review. (SFS 1983:370)

**Section 8**

Unless a provision of this chapter or of another law prescribes otherwise, an appeal from a lower court order may be brought only in conjunction with an appeal from a judgment or final order.

Even if a party has not appealed from a judgment or final order, in response to a demand of his adversary for a change in the judgment or final order, he may request review of an order which may not be appealed separately.

When separate appeal is not permitted from a court order issued on penalty of fine or specifying any other adverse consequence in the event of non-compliance, the person against whom the conditional order is directed may request review of its legality in conjunction with a separate appeal from the subsequent order reducing the conditional sanction to an unconditional obligation.

### Section 9

Review of a lower court order dismissing a notice of appeal from, a formal notice of exception to, an application for reopening or reinstatement of, or a regular or limited appeal from, the judgment or order of the lower court may be sought by limited appeal. Under no circumstances may a court of appeals review the question whether such notice was given, or application made, or appeal taken in the prescribed form and in due time.

### Section 10

The directions of the lower court as to the form of appeal must be followed.

### Section 11

If a party, pursuant to section 3, has given a formal notice of exception to a lower court order rendered in course of the proceedings, and has been directed to bring a separate appeal from the order, the proceedings shall be stayed pending the outcome of the appeal. If the court finds that the preparation of the case should be continued, however, it may so direct.

When a formal notice of exception pursuant to section 4 is given, the court, for special cause, may direct a stay of the proceedings pending the outcome of the appeal.

In situations other than those referred to above, no stay may be effected pending appeal from a lower court order rendered in the course of the proceedings.

# Chapter 50

## Regular Appeals in civil cases

### Section 1

A party desiring to take a regular appeal from a lower court judgment in a civil action shall give a notice of appeal to the lower court within one week of the pronouncement of the judgment. The court shall determine immediately whether or not the notice is proper.

A party who has given a notice of appeal shall perfect his appeal by submitting an appeal petition to the lower court within three weeks of the pronouncement of the judgment.

## Section 2

If a party has appealed from a lower court judgment pursuant to section 1, the adverse party, although he did not observe the provisions of the said section, may also appeal from the judgment; to do so, however, he must submit an appeal petition to the lower court within one week of the expiration of the time to appeal pursuant to section 1.

If the first appeal is withdrawn or otherwise terminates prior to adjudication on the merits, the later appeal also terminates.

## Section 3

If it is found that an appeal is not brought in the prescribed form or in due time, it shall be dismissed by the lower court. If a notice of appeal has been filed with the court of appeals before the expiration of the period for appeal, the fact that the notice was only subsequently filed with the lower court shall not be cause for its dismissal. (SFS 1973:240)

## Section 4

In the appeal petition the appellant shall specify:

1. the judgment appealed from;

2. the grounds for the appeal, stating the respect in which the appellant considers the fact findings and legal conclusions of the lower court to be erroneous; and

3. the particular part of the judgment attached and the change in the judgment demanded by the appellant.

In the petition the appellant shall specify the evidence upon which he desires to rely and indicate what he intends to prove by each specified item. The original or a certified copy of any document not previously presented shall be annexed to the petition. If the appellant desires that the court of appeals hear the testimony of a witness or an expert, or of a party under truth affirmation, or that the court of appeals view the locus in quo, he shall so state in the petition, indicating the reasons therefor. The appellant shall also state in the petition whether he desires the adverse party to appear in person at the main hearing in the court of appeals.

The petition shall be signed by the party or his attorney in his own hand. (SFS 1963:149)

## Section 5

If the appeal is not dismissed, upon expiration of the time stated in section 2 the lower court shall transmit without delay to the court of appeals the appeal petition with the papers annexed thereto and the case file.

If the petition contains a demand requiring immediate consideration, such as a request for provisional attachment or for the termination of such a measure, or for an order that execution of a judgment may occur forthwith, the transmission shall occur immediately upon receipt of the petition; however, until the time stated in section 2 has expired, a copy of the petition shall be held accessible at the lower court. (SFS 1981:828)

**Section 6**

If an impediment other than the kind referred to in section 3 precludes consideration of the appeal upon the merits, the appeal may be dismissed forthwith by the court of appeals.

**Section 7**

If the petition fails to comply with the regulations in section 4 or is otherwise incomplete, the court of appeals shall direct the appellant to cure the defect.

If the appellant fails to comply with a directive in accordance with the first paragraph, the petition shall be dismissed if it is so incomplete that it cannot without essential inconvenience be used as basis for the proceedings in the court of appeals. (SFS 1984:131)

**Section 8**

In order to commence preparation of the case on appeal, the petition with the papers annexed thereto shall be served upon the appellee with a notice directing him to file a written answer.

If it is manifest that the petition is unfounded, however, the court of appeals may immediately pass judgment without taking any measure as stated in the first paragraph.

If the lower court has denied a request for provisional attachment, or other measure according to chapter 15 or has ordered the termination of such a measure, the court of appeals may immediately grant the measure to remain effective until otherwise ordered. If the lower court has granted such a measure, or has directed that execution of a judgment may occur forthwith, the court of appeals may immediately direct that no further step be taken to implement the measure or to execute the order. (SFS 1984:131)

**Section 9**

Unless the appellant's demand for a change in the judgment is consented to, the answer shall contain the appellant's grounds for appeal and specify the circumstances upon which the appellee desires to rely.

In the answer the appellee shall specify the evidence upon which he desires to rely and indicate what he intends to prove by each specified item. The original or a certified copy of any document not previously presented shall be annexed to the answer. If the appellee desires that the court of appeals hear the testimony of a witness or an expert, or of a party under truth affirmation, or that the court of appeals view the locus in quo, he shall so state in the answer indicating the reasons therefor. The appellee shall also state in the answer whether he desires the adverse party to appear in person at the main hearing in the court of appeals.

The petition shall be signed by the appellant or his attorney in his own hand. (SFS 1963:149)

**Section 10**

The answers with the papers annexed thereto shall be served upon the appellant.

If it is found necessary for the preparation of the case, the court of appeals may direct a further exchange of writings. The court may also issue detailed regulations as to the exchange of writings and even particularize the issues upon which the parties shall express themselves. However, a party may be directed to file more than one writing only for special cause.

**Section 11**

If the court of appeals finds it necessary to obtain expert opinions, documents, or objects for view or inspection, or to take proof outside the main hearing or any other preparatory measure, it shall issue an order thereon without delay.

A party who desires that one of the measures referred to above be taken shall apply therefor to the court of appeals as soon as possible.

**Section 12**

If examination of a party or a third person is found necessary for the preparation of the case the court of appeals shall direct such examination in the manner it finds appropriate.

**Section 13**

As soon as the preparation of the case has been concluded, the court of appeals shall fix a date for the main hearing. A main hearing may be fixed for the disposition of a procedural issue, or of a portion of the controversy that may be decided separately, although in other respects the preparation of the case has not been completed.

### Section 14

Notice to attend the main hearing shall be given to the parties.

The appellant shall be directed to appear on pain that otherwise he forfeits his appeal. Moreover, if he is to appear in person, the court of appeals shall direct him to do so on penalty of fine. If the appellee is obliged to appear in person, or if his presence is otherwise found to be of importance for the disposition or investigation of the case, he shall be directed to appear on penalty of fine; when a conditional fine is not directed, the appellee shall be reminded that the case may be heard and decided notwithstanding his absence.

The court of appeals shall also decide whether a witness or expert shall be notified to appear at the main hearing. The parties shall be given notice of any direction issued for the attendance of a witness or an expert. As to notices to witnesses or experts to appear at the main hearing, the provisions in chapters 36 and 40 shall apply.

### Section 15

As to main hearings in other respects the provisions in chapter 1, section 9, and chapter 43, sections 1–6 and 10–13, shall correspondingly apply; however, with respect to notices to appear at postponed main hearings and directions for the parties, the provisions in section 14 of this chapter shall apply. (SFS 1969:244)

### Section 16

At the main hearing, the lower court judgment shall be read to the extent necessary, and the appellant shall state both the part of the judgment appealed from and his demand for a change in the judgment. The appellee shall indicate whether he consents to or opposes the demand.

Subsequently, unless the court of appeals finds another sequence more suitable, the appellant shall present his position, followed by the appellee. Each party shall respond to the allegations of his adversary. When the hearing is held despite the absence of the appellee, to the extent necessary his position shall be presented from the documents by the court.

The statements of an appearing party in the exchange of writings or otherwise during the preparation of the case may be read only if his oral testimony at the hearing departs from his earlier statement, or if he fails to testify, or if special cause otherwise warrants the reading of such prior statements.

**Section 17**

After the opening statements of the parties, the evidence shall be presented. When the main hearing is held despite absence of the appellee, to the extent necessary the evidence produced by him at the lower court shall be presented by the court of appeals.

In the absence of special cause for a different order of presentation, the evidence to be brought forward from protocols and other documents filed with the lower court should be presented before evidence concerning the same circumstance is taken directly by the court of appeals. When there are several evidentiary items concerning the same circumstance, they should be presented in sequence without interruption.

**Section 18**

After the evidence has been presented, the parties may state what they regard as necessary for the summation of their positions.

**Section 19**

If the appellant fails to appear at a main hearing his appeal shall be dismissed.

In an action not amenable to out of court settlement, if an appellee directed to appear on penalty of fine fails to appear, the court of appeals, in lieu of directing him to appear under the sanction of a new conditional fine, may direct that he be brought before it in custody either immediately or on the date to which the session has been adjourned.

In an action not amenable of out of court settlement, if a party directed to appear in person on penalty of fine appears by attorney only, the court of appeals, in lieu of directing him to appear under the sanction of a new conditional fine, may direct that he be brought before it in custody either immediately or on the date to which the session has been adjourned.

However, if a party has been directed to appear on penalty of fine, or if a party is to be brought before the court in custody and it is found that the order for bringing him to court cannot be executed, the appeal may be heard and decided on the merits notwithstanding the fact that the party has appeared by attorney only, or has failed to appear.

**Section 20**

If the appellant's appeal has become void pursuant to section 19 and he had a valid excuse for non-appearance which he could not notify in time, the court of appeals shall reinstate the case at his request.

An application for reinstatement shall be made in writing within two weeks of the date when the decision was notified. If the plaintiff again fails to appear, his right to reinstatement is forfeited. (SFS 1984:131)

**Section 21**

The court of appeals may dispose of an appeal on the merits without a main hearing,

1. if the appellant's claim is consented to,

2. if it is plain that the claim is unfounded,

3. if both parties have requested that the appeal be disposed of on the merits without a main hearing or have declared that they have no objection thereto, or

4. if the value of the claim on appeal is plainly less, at the time of the lower court's judgment, than the basic amount stated in the National Insurance Act (1962:381), unless both parties have requested a main hearing.

In computing the value as stated in the first paragraph, point 4, litigation costs and interest accrued after the commencement of the action are not taken into account.

An appeal may always be decided on the merits without a main hearing if it is plain that such a hearing is not required.

For the determination of a question not related to the substance of the appeal a main hearing is not required. (SFS 1984:131)

**Section 22**

If the court of appeals has ordered that a case shall be decided on the merits without a main hearing, and it is not obvious at the time of the order that the parties have already concluded their presentations, an opportunity to do so shall be given to them.

Notwithstanding any previous order, the court of appeals may direct that a main hearing shall be held. (SFS 1954:432)

**Section 23**

If testimony of a witness or an expert, or of a party under truth affirmation, was heard at the main hearing in the lower court with respect to a particular circumstance, or if a view concerning a certain fact was held during the main hearing in the lower court, and the evaluation of such evidence is decisive of the outcome on appeal, the relevant part of the lower courts judgment may not be changed by the court of appeals unless the appellate court hears or views the evidence anew, or extraordinary reasons justify the conclusion that the value of the evidence is other than that attached to it by the lower court.

**Section 24**

If a default judgment is attacked on appeal by the appearing party who requested such a judgment, and an application by the party in default for reopening is granted, the claim on appeal shall be remanded by the court of appeals to the lower court to be processed as part of the reopened case.

**Section 25**

An appeal may be withdrawn at any time prior to the pronouncement of the judgment or final order of the court of appeals.

An appellant may not amend his claim on appeal to include a part of the lower court judgment other than that specified in the appeal petition.

A party may assert in support of his position in the court of appeals a circumstance or evidence not previously presented only if he shows it to be probable that he had a valid excuse for his failure to rely upon the circumstance or evidence in the lower court, or if for any other reason the assertion of the circumstance or evidence should be allowed. A set-off defence initially asserted in the court of appeals may be dismissed unless it can be tried in the appellate proceeding without inconvenience. (SFS 1971:218)

**Section 26**

If a grave procedural error of the kind referred to in chapter 59, section 1, 1 to 4, occurred in the lower court, the court of appeals shall vacate the lower court judgment even if not requested to do so.

If a grave procedural error of another kind occurred in the lower court, for cause, the court of appeals may vacate the judgment even if not requested to do so.

The judgment may be vacated in whole or only in part. If the procedural error also affects a part of the judgment from which no appeal has been taken, the court of appeals shall determine, based upon the particular circumstances, whether that part shall be vacated.

**Section 27**

If the issue of the disqualification of a judge in the lower court is raised in conjunction with an appeal from the judgment, and the complaint is well-founded, the court of appeals shall vacate the lower court judgment to the extent appealed from.

### Section 28

If a procedural error other than those referred to in section 26 or 27 is alleged, the appellate court may vacate the lower court judgment only if the error can be assumed to have affected the outcome of the case and correction of the error cannot be accomplished in the appellant court without substantial inconvenience.

### Section 29

If the court of appeals vacates a lower court judgment, and the decision on appeal is not based on lack of competence in the court below or another ground indicating that the lower court should not have entertained the case on the merits, the court of appeals shall remand the case to the lower court for the required further processing.

The authority of the court of appeals, when it finds that the court below lacked competence, to refer the case to another lower court is prescribed in chapter 10, section 20.

### Section 30

After the judgment or final order of the court of appeals has become conclusive, the file received from the lower court and a copy of the judgment or order on appeal shall be transmitted to the lower court.

## Chapter 51

### Regular Appeals in Criminal Cases

### Section 1

A party desiring to take a regular appeal from a lower court judgment in a criminal action shall submit an appeal petition to the lower court within three weeks of the pronouncement of the judgment.

### Section 2

If a party has appealed from a lower court judgment pursuant to section 1, the adverse party, although he did not observe the provisions of the said section, may also appeal from the judgment; to do so, however, he must submit an appeal petition to the lower court within one week of the expiration of the time to appeal pursuant to section 1.

If the first appeal is withdrawn or otherwise terminated prior to adjudication on the merits, the later appeal also terminates.

## Section 3

IF it is found that an appeal is not brought in the prescribed form or in due time, it shall be dismissed by the lower court. If a notice of appeal has been filed with the court of appeals before the expiration of the period for appeal, the fact that the notice was only subsequently filed with the lower court shall not be cause for its dismissal. (SFS 1973:240)

## Section 4

In the appeal petition the appellant shall specify:

1. the judgment appealed from;

2. the grounds for the appeal, stating the respect in which the appellant considers the fact findings and legal conclusions of the lower court to be erroncous; and

3. the particular part of the judgment attacked and the change in the judgment demanded by the appellant.

In the petition the appellant shall specify the evidence upon which he desires to rely and indicate what he intends to prove by each specified item. The original or a certified copy of any document not previously presented shall be annexed to the petition. If the appellant desires that the court of appeals hear the testimony of a witness or an expert, or view the locus in quo, he shall so state in the petition, indicating the reasons therefor. The appellant shall also state in the petition whether he desires the injured person or the defendant to appear in person at the main hearing in the court of appeals.

When the defendant is under arrest or in detention, this information shall be stated in the appeal petition.

The petition shall be signed by the appellant or his attorney in his own hand. (SFS 1963:149)

## Section 5

If the appeal is not dismissed, upon expiration of the time stated in section 2 the lower court shall transmit without delay to the court of appeals the appealed petition with the papers annexed thereto and the case file.

If the defendant is in detention, or if the petition contains a demand requiring immediate consideration, such as a request for the detention of the defendant, or for a measure referred to in chapters 25 to 28, or for the termination of such a measure, the transmission shall occur immediately upon receipt of the petition; however, until the time stated in section 2 has expired, a copy of the petition shall be held accessible at the lower court. (SFS 1947:616)

## Section 6

If an impediment other than the kind referred to in section 3 precludes consideration of the appeal on the merits, the appeal may be dismissed forthwith by the court of appeals.

## Section 7

If the petition fails to comply with the regulations in section 4, or is otherwise incomplete, the court of appeals shall direct the appellant to cure the defect.

If the appellant fails to comply with a directive as stated in the first paragraph, the appeal shall be dismissed if the petition is so incomplete that it cannot without essential inconvenience be used as basis for the proceedings in the court of appeals. (SFS 1984:131)

## Section 8

In order to commence preparation of the case on appeal, the petition with the papers annexed thereto shall be served upon the appellee with a notice directing him to file a written answer.

If the petition is plainly unfounded, however, the court of appeals may immediately pass judgment without taking any action as stated in the first paragraph.

If the lower court has denied a request for a measure stated in chapters 26 to 28, or ordered the termination of such a measure, the court of appeals may immediately grant the measure to remain effective until otherwise ordered. If the lower court has granted such a measure, the court of appeals may immediately direct that no further step be taken to execute the lower court order. As to detention and travel prohibition, the court of appeals may also change the lower court order without giving the adverse party an opportunity to be heard. (SFS 1984:131)

## Section 9

The answer shall contain the appellant's grounds for his appeal and specify the circumstances upon which the appellee desires to rely.

In the answer the appellee shall specify the evidence upon which he desires to rely and indicate what he intends to prove by each specified item. The original or a certified copy of any document not previously presented shall be annexed to the answer. If the appellee desires that the court of appeals hear the testimony of a witness or an expert, or view the locus in quo, he shall so state in his answer, indicating his reasons therefor. The appellee shall also state in his answer whether he desires the injured person or the defendant to appear in person at the main hearing in the court of appeal.

The answer shall be signed personally by the appellee or his attorney or, when the defendant is the appellee, by his defence counsel. (SFS 1963:149)

**Section 10**

The answer with the papers annexed thereto shall be served upon the appellant.

If it is found necessary for the preparation of the case, the court of appeals may direct a further exchange of writings. The court may also issue detailed regulations as to the exchange of writings and even particularize the issues upon which the parties shall express themselves. However, a party may be directed to file more than one writing only for special cause.

**Section 11**

If the court of appeals finds it necessary to obtain expert opinions, documents, or objects for view or inspection, or to take proof outside the main hearing or any other preparatory measure, it shall issue an order thereon without delay.

A party who desires that one of the measures referred to above be taken shall apply therefor to the court of appeals as soon as possible.

In a public prosecution, if it is found that the preliminary investigation should be expanded or, if no investigation was made, that such an investigation should take place, the court of appeals may direct the prosecutor accordingly.

**Section 12**

If examination of a party or a third person is found necessary for the preparation of the case, the court of appeals shall direct such examination in the manner it finds appropriate. As to the appearance in court of a defendant who is under arrest or in detention, the court of appeals shall issue the appropriate directive to provide for his presence.

**Section 13**

As soon as the preparation of the case has been concluded, the court of appeals shall fix a date for the main hearing. A main hearing may be fixed for the disposition of a procedural issue, or of a portion of the controversy that may be decided separately, although in other respects the preparation of the case has not been completed.

If the defendant is in detention, the main hearing shall be held within four weeks of the expiration of the time stated in section 2, unless a longer postponement is necessary owing to a measure referred to in section 11 or to another circumstance. If the defendant was detained after the expiration of the time stated in section 2, the period shall be computed from the day of his detention.

**Section 14**

The parties shall be summoned to appear at the main hearing.

A private appellant shall be directed to appear on pain that he otherwise forfeits his appeal. Moreover, if he is to appear in person, he shall be reminded of the provision in section 19, first paragraph, second sentence. If a private appellant is obliged to appear in person, or if his presence is otherwise found to be of importance for the disposition or investigation of the case, he shall be directed to appear on penalty of fine. If there is cause to believe that the defendant would not comply with such direction, the court of appeals may ordain that he be brought before it in custody. If no such direction or ordination is given, the defendant shall be reminded that the case may be decided notwithstanding his absence. As to the appearance of a defendant who is under arrest or in detention, the court of appeals shall issue the appropriate directive to provide for his presence.

In a public prosecution, if the injured person is to be examined as part of the prosecutor's case, he shall be directed to appear in person at the main hearing on penalty of fine.

The court of appeals shall also decide whether a witness or an expert shall be notified to appear at the main hearing. The parties shall be given notice of any direction issued for the attendance of a witness or an expert. As to notices to witnesses or experts to appear at the main hearing, the provisions in chapters 36 and 40 shall apply.(SFS 1984:131)

**Section 15**

As to main hearings in other respects the provisions in chapter 1, section 9, and chapter 46, sections 1–5, 7, 9, 11, 13 and 16, shall correspondingly apply; however, with respect to notices to appear at postponed main hearings and to directions for the parties, the provisions in section 14 of this chapter shall apply.

When a case is scheduled for a continued or new main hearing, the court of appeals may direct the measures found appropriate to facilitate conclusion of the case at that hearing.

As to such measures the provisions in sections 10–12 of this chapter shall apply. (SFS 1969:244)

**Section 16**

At the main hearing the lower court judgment shall be read to the extent necessary, and the appellant shall state both the part of the judgment appealed from and his demand for a change in the judgment. The appellee shall be given an opportunity to respond to the demand.

Subsequently, the prosecutor, or the injured person, if he is the sole appellant on the prosecution's side, shall present the position of the prosecution to the extent required for the trial at the appellate level. If the defendant has appealed, however, and the court of appeals finds it more suitable, the defendant may present his position first, followed by the prosecutor of the injured person. Each party shall be given an opportunity to respond to the allegations of his adversary. When the hearing is held despite the absence of the appellee, to the extent necessary, his position shall be presented from the documents by the court.

During the examination of the injured person or of the defendant, the written record of his prior statements made before the lower court, a prosecutor, or a police authority may be read only if his oral testimony departs from his earlier statement, or if he fails to testify.

**Section 17**

After the opening statements of the parties, the evidence shall be presented. The evidence presented in the lower court, to the extent that it is of importance for the appeal, shall be presented by the court of appeals in the state in which it appears in the protocol and other documents; however, when the court of appeals finds it more suitable and the parties consent thereto, the evidence from the proceedings below may be presented by the parties.

In the absence of special cause for a different order of presentation, the evidence to be brought forward from protocol and other documents filed with the lower court should be presented before evidence concerning the same circumstance is taken directly by the court of appeals. When there are several evidentiary items concerning the same circumstance, they should be presented in sequence without interruption.

**Section 18**

After the evidence has been presented, the parties may state what they regard as necessary for the summation of their positions.

**Section 19**

If a private appellant fails to appear at a main hearing, his appeal shall be dismissed. The same applies if a private appellant, who has been instructed to appear in person, appears only by proxy and the court of appeals does not consider it can nevertheless decide the case.

If a private appellee directed to appear on penalty of fine fails to appear, the court of appeals, in lieu of directing him to appear under penalty of a new fine, may direct that he be brought before it in custody, either immediately or on a later date. The same applies if a private appellee directed to appear in person on penalty of fine appears only by proxy.

In a public prosecution, if an injured party who is to be examined in support of the prosecution fails to appear in person, the rule in the second paragraph shall apply.

If the appellee has been directed to appear on penalty of fine, or if he is to be brought before the court in custody and the order to do so cannot be executed, the court of appeals may decide the case on the merits notwithstanding the fact that the appellee has appeared only by proxy or has failed to appear. A case may also be decided on the merits if a private appellant who has been directed to appear in person appears only by proxy. (SFS 1984:131)

**Section 20**

If the appeal has been dismissed pursuant to section 19 and the appellant had a valid excuse for his absence or failure to appear which he was unable to notify in time, the court of appeals shall reinstate the case at his request.

The application for reinstatement shall be made in writing within two weeks of the issuance of the dismissal order. If, after reinstatement of the case, the appellant fails to appear at the main hearing or to comply with a directive to appear in person, his right to reinstatement of the case shall be forfeited. (SFS 1984:131)

**Section 21**

The court of appeals may dispose of an appeal on the merits without a main hearing,

1. if the prosecutor appeals only for the benefit of the defendant,

2. if an appeal brought by the defendant is supported by the adverse party,

3. if the appeal is plainly unfounded, or

4. if no cause exists to hold the defendant legally liable, or to impose a sanction upon him, or to impose a sanction other than fine or conditional sentence, or a concurrence of such sanctions.

On an equality with the sanctions stated in the first paragraph, 4, are sentencing to a fine and, if it is not at the same time a question of forfeiting of conditionally granted freedom from imprisonment, an order in accordance with Chapter 34, Section 1, first paragraph, 1, of the Penal Code.

If, as stated in the first paragraph, a party has requested a main hearing, this shall take place unless manifestly unnecessary.

If a prosecution is brought for other than legal liability, the case may be decided without a main hearing only if, pursuant to Chapter 50, Section 21, the case may be tried without a main hearing.

For a ruling not relating to the actual matter in dispute a main hearing need not take place. (SFS 1984:131)

**Section 22**

If the court of appeals has ordered that a case shall be decided on the merits without a main hearing, and it is not obvious at the time of the order that the parties have already concluded their presentations, an opportunity to do so shall be given to them.

Notwithstanding any previous order, the court of appeals may direct that a main hearing shall be held. (SFS 1954:432)

**Section 23**

If testimony of a witness or an expert was heard at the main hearing in the lower court with respect to a particular circumstance, or if a view concerning a certain fact was held during the main hearing in the lower court, and the evaluation of such evidence is decisive of the outcome on appeal, the relevant part of the lower court judgment may not be changed by the court of appeals, except for the benefit of the defendant, unless the appellate court hears or views the evidence anew, or extraordinary reasons justify the conclusion that the value of the evidence is other than that attached to it by the lower court.

**Section 24**

An appeal may be withdrawn at any time prior to the pronouncement of the judgment or final order of the court of appeals. A prosecutor who appealed to the court of appeals against the defendant may amend his appeal to benefit the defendant.

An appellant may not amend his claim on appeal to include a criminal act other than the one specified in the appeal petition.

**Section 25**

In an appeal lodged by the defendant, or by the prosecutor for the benefit of the defendant, the court of appeals may not sentence the defendant to a criminal sanction more severe than the one imposed by the lower court. If the defendant was sentenced by the lower court to imprisonment, the court of appeals may order suspension of sentence, probation or surrender for special care; in addition to suspension of sentence and to probation or surrender for care within the social service, the court of appeals may impose a fine or probation coupled with imprisonment pursuant to chapter 28, section 3, of the Penal Code. When the lower court has ordered a sanction of the kind referred to above, the court of appeals may impose a different sanction. (SFS 1981:228)

**Section 26**

If a grave procedural error of the kind referred to in chapter 59, section 1, 1–4, occurred in the lower court, the court of appeals shall vacate the lower court judgment even if not requested to do so.

If a grave procedural error of another kind occurred in the lower court, for cause, the court of appeals may vacate the judgment even if not requested to do so.

The judgment may be vacated in whole or only in part. If the procedural error also affects a part of the judgment from which no appeal has been taken, the court of appeals shall determine, based upon the particular circumstances, whether that part shall be vacated.

**Section 27**

If the issue of the disqualification of a judge in the lower court is raised in conjunction with an appeal from the judgment, and the complaint is well-founded, the court of appeals shall vacate the lower court judgment to the extent appealed from.

**Section 28**

If the court of appeals finds a procedural error other than those referred to in section 26 or 27 to have occurred, the appellate court may vacate the lower court judgment only if the error can be assumed to have affected the outcome of the case, and correction of the error cannot be accomplished in the appellate court without substantial inconvenience.

**Section 29**

If the court of appeals vacates a lower court judgment, and the decision on appeal is not based on lack of competence in the court below or another ground indicating that the lower court should not have entertained the case on the merits, the court of appeals shall remand the case to the lower court for the required further processing.

The authority of the court of appeals, when it finds that the court below lacked competence, to refer the case to another lower court is described in chapter 19, section 11.

### Section 30

After a judgment or final order of a court of appeals has become conclusive, the file received from the lower court and a copy of the judgment or order on appeal shall be transmitted to the lower court.

### Section 31

When the appeal from the lower court judgment concerns only matters other than criminal liability, the case shall be disposed of in the court of appeals as a civil case.

## Chapter 52

### Limited Appeals

### Section 1

A person desiring to take a limited appeal from a lower court order shall submit a limited appeal petition to the lower court within two weeks of the pronouncement of the challenged order. However, if an order was rendered in the course of the proceedings, but not at a hearing session, and it was not announced during any such session when the order was to be issued, the period for appeal shall be computed from service of the order upon the complainant. No time limit shall apply to an appeal from an order requiring a person to be placed or kept in detention, or an order prohibiting him to travel, or an order on an issue as referred to in chapter 49, section 6.

The obligation to give a formal notice of exception to orders as referred to in chapter 49, section 3 or section 4, first paragraph, 1, 2, 3, 7, 8 or 9, is prescribed in the said chapter. (SFS 1984:131)

### Section 2

If it is found that a limited appeal is not brought in the prescribed form or in due time, it shall be dismissed by the lower court. If a notice of appeal has been filed with the court of appeals before the expiration of the period for appeal, the fact that the notice was only subsequently filed with the lower court shall not be cause for its dismissal. (SFS 1973:240)

### Section 3

In the limited appeal petition the complainant shall specify:

1. the order appealed from;
2. the grounds for the limited appeal; and

3. the change in the order demanded by the complainant.

In the petition, the complainant shall specify the evidence upon which he desires to rely and indicate what he intends to prove by each specified item. The original or a certified copy of any document not previously presented shall be annexed to the petition.

The petition shall be signed by the complainant or his attorney in his own hand. (SFS 1963:149)

**Section 4**

If the appeal is not dismissed, the lower court shall transmit without delay to the court of appeals the limited appeal petition with the papers annexed thereto and an original or certified copy of the file to the extent related to the challenged matter.

**Section 5**

If an impediment other than the kind referred to in section 2 precludes consideration of the appeal on the merits, the appeal may be dismissed forthwith by the court of appeals.

**Section 6**

If the petition fails to comply with the regulations in section 3 or is otherwise incomplete, the court of appeals shall direct the complainant to cure the defect.

If the complainant fails to comply with a directive as stated in the first paragraph, the limited appeal shall be dismissed if the petition is so incomplete that it cannot without essential inconvenience be used as basis for the proceedings in the court of appeals. (SFS 1984:131)

**Section 7**

If it is found that the adverse party should be given an opportunity to respond, the petition with the papers annexed thereto shall be served upon him with a notice directing him to file a written answer.

Unless an opportunity to respond has been given to the adverse party, the lower court order may not be changed to his detriment.

If the lower court, in a civil case, has denied a request for provisional attachment, or other measure according to chapter 15, or has ordered the termination of such a measure, or in a criminal case has denied a request for a measure stated in chapters 26–28, or has ordered the termination of such a measure, the court of appeals may immediately grant the measure to remain effective until otherwise ordered. If the lower court has granted such a measure, or has directed that execution of an order may occur forthwith, the court of appeals may immediately direct that no further step be taken to implement the measure or to execute the order. As to detention or travel prohibition, the appellate court may also change the lower court order without giving the adverse party an opportunity to answer. (SFS 1981:828)

**Section 8**

The answer shall respond to the complainant's grounds for his appeal and specify the circumstances upon which the respondent desires to rely.

The respondent shall specify the evidence upon which he desires to rely, and indicate what he intends to prove by each specified item. The original or a certified copy of any document not previously presented shall be annexed to the answer.

The answer shall be signed personally by the respondent or his attorney or, in a criminal case in which the defendant is the respondent, by his defence counsel. (SFS 1963:149)

**Section 9**

After an answer is filed, if the court of appeals finds that a further exchange of writings is necessary, it may so direct. The court may also issue detailed regulations as to the exchange of writings and even particularize the issues upon which the parties shall express themselves. However, a party may be directed to file more than one writing only for special cause.

**Section 10**

If examination of a party or a third person is found necessary for the investigation, the court of appeals shall direct such examination in the manner it finds appropriate. As to the appearance in court of a defendant who is under arrest or in detention, the court of appeals shall issue the appropriate directive to provide for his presence.

**Section 11**

After the required measures have been taken, the appeal shall be decided by the court of appeals as soon as possible.

**Section 12**

A limited appeal may be withdrawn at any time prior to the pronouncement of the final order by the court of appeals.

**Section 13**

After the final order of the court of appeals has become conclusive, the file received from the lower court and a copy of the order on appeal shall be transmitted to the lower court.

## Chapter 53

### Actions Commenced in Court of Appeals

#### Section 1

In a civil action instituted in a court of appeals as a court of first instance, the provisions of chapters 42–44 concerning proceedings in the lower courts shall correspondingly apply.

#### Section 2

In a criminal case instituted in a court of appeals as a court of first instance, the provisions in chapters 45–47 concerning proceedings in the lower courts shall correspondingly apply; however, in such a case, the following diverging provisions shall govern:

1. The court of appeals may not authorize the prosecutor to issue a summons.

2. For the preparation of the action, the court of appeals may direct the defendant in the summons to file a written answer with the court. The answer with the papers annexed thereto shall be served upon the prosecutor. When a further exchange of writings is found necessary for the preparation of the action, the court of appeals may so direct. The court may also issue detailed regulations as to the exchange of writings and even particularize the issues upon which the parties shall express themselves.

3. In lieu of the one week period prescribed in chapter 45, section 14, chapter 46, section 11 and chapter 47, section 22, for holding the main hearing in cases in which the defendant is under arrest or in detention, a period of two weeks shall apply.

4. If there is no cause to sentence the defendant to punishment more severe than fine, the court of appeals may decide the case on the merits without a main hearing; as to such a decision, the provisions in chapter 51, section 22, shall govern. (SFS 1964:166).

# Part Six

# Proceedings in the Supreme Court

## Chapter 54

### Appeals from Judgments and Orders of the Courts of Appeals

#### Section 1

Appeal from a court of appeals judgment shall be sought by a review petition.

A party against whom a default judgment was entered may not appeal from the judgment; his right to a reopening of the case following the entry of such a judgment is prescribed in chapter 44, section 9, and chapter 53, section 1.

In an action amenable to out of court settlement, if a party has undertaken not to appeal from the judgment after the controversy arose, the undertaking shall be given effect; however, a commitment prior to the entry of judgment shall not be effective unless a reciprocal undertaking was made by the adverse party.

#### Section 2

Appeal from a court of appeals final order shall be sought by limited appeal. However, when an order dismissing a specified part of a case without reaching the merits is issued in conjunction with a judgment, review of the order shall be sought by a review petition.

A party entitled to apply for reinstatement of a case terminated by a final order may not appeal from the order.

#### Section 3

The provisions in chapter 49, sections 3–5, 7 and 11, concerning appeals from lower court orders shall correspondingly apply to appeals from orders, other than final orders, of the courts of appeals on issues referred to in the said sections and raised in, or appealed to, the appellate courts.

**Section 4**

As to orders of the courts of appeals other than those referred to in the preceding sections, the provisions in chapter 49, section 8, shall govern.

**Section 5**

As to an order of the court of appeals denying a request for detention or travel prohibition, or releasing a detained person, or terminating a travel prohibition, an appeal may be brought only in conjunction with an appeal from a judgment or final order of the appellate court.

**Section 6**

A court of appeals order remanding a case to the lower court is not reviewable; however, as an exception to this proscription, if the disposition by the court of appeals embraces decision of a question that bears directly upon the ultimate outcome of the action, an immediate appeal may be sought.

**Section 7**

A ruling of a court of appeals that the lower court is competent to entertain a case is not reviewable unless the challenge to the competence of the lower court is based upon a ground that the higher courts, on appeal, are required to notice on their own motion.

**Section 8**

A court of appeals order concerning the disqualification of a judge in the lower court or with respect to the lower court disposition of an issue as referred to in chapter 49, section 4, first paragraph, 7 or 9, or section 6, is not subject to review. (SFS 1979:242)

**Section 9**

An appeal from a court of appeals judgment or final order in a case or non-contentious proceeding initiated at a lower court may not be considered by the Supreme Court to a further extent than prescribed in section 10 unless the Supreme Court has granted the party review dispensation.

However, in a case involving public prosecution, this rule does not apply to an appeal brought by the Chief State Prosecutor, the Attorney General or a Parliamentary Ombudsman. (SFS 1968:79)

**Section 10**

Review Dispensation may be granted only if

1. for guidance in application of the law it is of importance that the Supreme Court decide the case; or

2. extraordinary cause exists for such review, such as that a ground exists for relief for substantive defects or that there has been a grave procedural error or that the outcome of the case in the court of appeals was plainly due to a gross oversight or a gross mistake.

If review dispensation is granted in one of two or more similar cases that are justiciable simultaneously, review dispensation may be granted also in the other cases. (SFS 1971:218)

**Section 11**

Review dispensation may be limited to a specified part of the judgment or final order to which the appeal relates. Pending its review of the case in that respect the Supreme Court may stay proceedings in respect of review dispensation for another portion of the case.

If review dispensation is granted with such limitation as is referred to in the first paragraph, it shall apply to the judgment or the final order in its entirety, if the party appeals therefrom, as well as to an order which is appealed from in conjunction with the appeal from the judgment or final order.

Insofar as review dispensation is not granted and proceedings relating thereto are not stayed, the judgment or final order of the court of appeals shall be immune to attack. A notification to that effect shall be included in the Supreme court's order. (SFS 1971:218)

**Section 12**

When deciding whether review dispensation shall be granted, consideration need be taken solely of circumstances asserted by the appellant. (SFS 1981:1088)

**Section 13**

As to an appeal from an order of a court of appeals other than a final order in a case or non-contentious judicial proceeding initiated in a lower court, the provisions in section 9–12 shall apply unless, by reason of an appeal from the judgment or final order, of the court of appeals, review dispensation has been granted which, pursuant to section 11, second paragraph, applies also to the order. (SFS 1981:1088)

**Section 14**

When a court of appeals issues an order which, pursuant to section 5, 6, 7 or 8, is not subject to review on appeal to the Supreme Court, the court of appeals shall so state in the order.

If an appeal from a court of appeals judgment or order cannot be entertained by the Supreme Court unless the latter grants review dispensation to the party, the court of appeals shall so state in its appeal instruction, with notification of the contents of section 10. (SFS 1971:218)

### Section 15

A party who considers an instruction issued by the court of appeals pursuant to section 14 to be erroneous may request review of the instruction in conjunction with an appeal from the judgment or order.

Questions referred to in the first paragraph may not be raise in the Supreme Court except as there stated. In all other respects the directions of the court of appeals as to the form of appeal must be followed. (SFS 1971:218)

### Section 16

Review of a court of appeals order dismissing a formal notice of exception to, an application for reopening or reinstatement of, or a regular or limited appeal from, the judgment or order of the court of appeals may be sought by limited appeal. Under no other circumstances may the Supreme Court review the question whether such notice was given or application made, or appeal taken in the prescribed form and in due time.

### Section 17–19

Repealed by SFS 1971:218.

## Chapter 55

### Regular Appeals to the Supreme Court

### Section 1

A party desiring to take a regular appeal from a court of appeals judgment shall submit a review petition to the appellate court within four weeks of the pronouncement of the judgment.

### Section 2

Repealed by SFS 1971:218.

**Section 3**

If it is found that an appeal is not brought in the prescribed form or in due time, it shall be dismissed by the court of appeals. If a review petition has been filed with the Supreme Court before the expiration of the period for appeal, the fact that the petition was only subsequently filed with the court of appeals shall not be cause for its dismissal. (SFS 1973:240)

**Section 4**

In the review petition the appellant shall specify

1. the judgment appealed from;

2. the grounds for the appeal, stating the respect in which the appellant considers the fact findings and legal conclusions of the court of appeals to be erroneous, and

3. the particular part of the judgment attacked and the change in the judgment demanded by the appellant.

If the appellant requests review dispensation, he shall specify in the petition the circumstances he relies upon in support thereof.

In the petition the appellant shall specify the evidence upon which he desires to rely and indicate what he intends to prove by each specified item. In a civil case, if evidence is specified which was not presented previously the appellant shall state why the evidence was not offered at an earlier stage. The original or a certified copy of any documentary evidence not previously presented shall be annexed to the petition. The appellant shall also state in the petition whether he desires the adverse party or, in a criminal case, the injured person or the defendant to appear in person at the main hearing in the Supreme Court.

In criminal cases, if the defendant is under arrest or in detention, this shall be stated in the petition.

The petition shall be signed by the party or his attorney in his own hand. (SFS 1981:1088)

**Section 5**

If the appeal is not dismissed, upon expiration of the time stated in section 1 the court of appeals shall transmit without delay to the Supreme Court the review petition with the papers annexed thereto and the case files of the lower court and the appellate court.

The transmission shall occur immediately on receipt of the petition in criminal cases, if the defendant is in detention, or in any case in which the petition contains a demand requiring immediate consideration, such as a request in civil cases for provisional attachment or injunction against dissipation, or for the termination of such a measure, or for an order that execution may occur forthwith, or a request in criminal cases for the detention of the defendant, or for a measure stated in chapters 25–28, or for the termination of such a measure. (SFS 1947:616)

**Section 6**

If an impediment other than the kind referred to in section 3 precludes consideration of the appeal upon the merits, the appeal may be dismissed forthwith by the Supreme Court.

**Section 7**

If the review petition fails to comply with the regulations in section 4, first, third or fifth paragraph, or is otherwise incomplete, the Supreme Court shall direct the appellant to cure the defect.

If the appellant fails to comply with a directive as stated in the first paragraph, the appeal shall be dismissed if the petition is so incomplete that it cannot without essential inconvenience be used as basis for the proceedings in the Supreme Court. (SFS 1984:131)

**Section 8**

In order to commence preparation of the case, the petition with the papers annexed thereto shall be served upon the appellee with a notice directing him to file a written answer.

If the court of appeals in a civil case has denied a request for provisional attachment, injunction against dissipation or any other security measure, or for an interlocutory decree, or has ordered the termination of such a measure or in a criminal case had denied a request for a measure stated in chapters 26–28, or has ordered the termination of such a measure, the Supreme Court may immediately grant the measure to remain effective until otherwise ordered. If the court of appeals has granted such a measure, or has directed that execution of a judgment may occur forthwith, or has confirmed a lower court order granting such a measure or authorizing immediate execution of a judgment the Supreme Court may immediately direct that no further step be taken to implement the measure or to execute the order. As to detention or travel prohibition the Supreme Court may also change the order of the court of appeals without giving the adverse party an opportunity to be heard.

**Section 9**

Unless in a civil case the appellant's demand for a change in the judgment is consented to, the answer shall contain the appellant's grounds for his appeal and specify the circumstances upon which the appellee desires to rely.

In the answer the appellee shall specify the evidence upon which he desires to rely and indicate what he intends to prove by each specified item. In a civil case, if evidence is specified which was not presented below, the appellee shall state why such evidence was not offered at an earlier stage. The original or a certified copy of any document not previously presented shall be annexed to the answer. The appellee shall also state in the answer whether he desires the adverse party or, in criminal cases, the injured person or the defendant to appear in person at the main hearing in the Supreme Court.

The answer shall be signed personally by the appellee or his attorney or, in criminal cases when the defendant is the appellee, by his defence counsel. (SFS 1963:149)

**Section 10**

The answer with the papers annexed thereto shall be served upon the appellant.

If it is found necessary for the preparation of the case, the Supreme Court may direct a further exchange of writings. The court may also issue detailed regulations as to the exchange of writings and even particularize the issues upon which the parties shall express themselves. However, a party may be directed to file more than one writing only for special cause.

**Section 11**

If review dispensation is required, after the conclusion of the exchange of writings the Supreme Court shall determine whether such dispensation shall be granted. For cause, the matter of dispensation may be disposed of, although an exchange of writings has not occurred. (SFS 1981:1088)

**Section 12**

The Supreme Court may dispose of an appeal on the merits without a main hearing if the action was immediately taken up for adjudication in the court of appeals.

When an appeal or a certain issue arising therein is to be decided by the Supreme Court en banc, a main hearing is not required.

As regards a decision in other respects by the Supreme Court without main hearing the provisions of Chapter 50, Section 21, shall be applicable in civil actions and of Chapter 51, Section 21, in criminal cases. (SFS 1984:131)

### Section 13

In civil cases a party may not assert in the Supreme Court in support of his position a circumstance or evidence not previously presented, unless he makes it appear probable that he was unable to claim the circumstance or evidence at a court below or that on other grounds he had a valid excuse for failing to do so. A set-off defence initially asserted in the Supreme Court may be dismissed unless it can be tried in the proceeding there without inconvenience.

### Section 14

If testimony of a witness or an expert, or of a party under truth affirmation was heard at the main hearing in a court below with respect to a particular circumstance, or if a view concerning a certain fact was held during the main hearing in a court below, and the evaluation of such evidence is decisive of the outcome in the Supreme Court, the relevant part of the court of appeals judgment may not be changed by the Supreme Court, except for the benefit of the defendant in a criminal case, unless the court of appeals, even if the evidence was not taken at a main hearing in that court, has changed the relevant portion of the lower court judgment, or extraordinary reasons justify the conclusion that the value of the evidence is other than that attached to it by the appellate court.

### Section 15

As to the proceedings in the Supreme Court in other respects, in civil cases chapter 50, sections 11–20, 22, 24 and 25, first and second paragraphs, and in criminal cases chapter 51, sections 11–20, 22, 24, 25 and 31, shall correspondingly apply.

The provisions concerning the vacation and remand of lower court judgments by the courts of appeals, with respect to civil cases chapter 50, sections 26–29, and with respect to criminal cases chapter 51, sections 26–29, shall correspondingly apply to vacation and remand of the judgment below by the Supreme Court.

### Section 16

After the Supreme Court has entered a judgment or final order, the files received from the court of appeals and copies of the judgment or order of the Supreme Court shall be returned, the court of appeals file to the appellate court and the lower court file to that court.

## Chapter 56

### Limited Appeal

#### Section 1

A person desiring to take a limited appeal from a court of appeals order shall submit a limited appeal petition to the appellate court within four weeks of the pronouncement of the challenged order; however, as to an order rendered in the course of the proceedings, but not at a hearing session, the period for appeal shall be computed from the date of service of the order upon the complainant. No time limit shall apply to an appeal from an order requiring a person to the placed or kept in detention or an order prohibiting him to travel.

The obligation to give formal notice of exception to orders as referred to in chapter 49, section 3 or section 4, first paragraph, 1, 2, 3, 7, 8 or 9, is prescribed in chapter 54, section 3. (SFS 1981:1294)

#### Section 2

Repealed by SFS 1971:218.

#### Section 3

If it is found that a limited appeal is not brought in the prescribed form or in due time, it shall be dismissed by the court of appeals. If an appeal petition has been filed with the Supreme Court before the expiration of the period for appeal, the fact that it was filed with the court of appeals only subsequently thereto shall not be cause for its dismissal. (SFS 1973:240)

#### Section 4

In the limited appeal petition the complainant shall specify:

1. the order appealed from;
2. the grounds for the limited appeal; and
3. the change in the order demanded by the complainant.

If the complainant requests review dispensation, he shall specify in the petition the circumstances he relies upon in support thereof.

In the petition the complainant shall specify the evidence upon which he desires to rely and indicate what he intends to prove by each specified item. The original or a certified copy of any documentary evidence shall be annexed to the petition.

The petition shall be signed by the complainant or his attorney in his own hand. (SFS 1981:1088)

### Section 5

If the appeal is not dismissed, the court of appeals shall transmit without delay to the Supreme Court the limited appeal petition with the papers annexed thereto, and the files of the lower and appellate courts or certified copies thereof, to the extent related to the challenged matter.

### Section 6

If an impediment other than the kind referred to in section 3 precludes consideration of the appeal upon the merits, the appeal may be dismissed forthwith by the Supreme Court.

### Section 7

If the limited appeal petition fails to comply with the regulations in section 4, first, second or fourth paragraph or is otherwise incomplete, the Supreme Court shall direct the complainant to cure the defect.

If the complainant fails to comply with a directive as stated in the first paragraph, the limited appeal shall be dismissed if the petition is so incomplete that it cannot without essential inconvenience be used as basis for the proceedings in the Supreme Court. (SFS 1984:131)

### Section 8

If it is found that the adverse party should be given an opportunity to respond, the petition with the papers annexed thereto shall be served upon him with a notice directing him to file a written answer.

### Section 9

The answer shall contain the complainant's grounds for his appeal and specify the circumstances upon which the respondent desires to rely.

The respondent shall specify the evidence upon which he desires to rely and indicate what he intends to prove by each specified item. The original or a certified copy of any document not previously presented shall be annexed to the answer.

The answer shall be signed personally by the respondent or his attorney or, in criminal cases, when the defendant is the respondent, by his defence counsel. (SFS 1963:149)

### Section 10

After an answer is filed, if the Supreme Court finds that a further exchange of writings is necessary, it may so direct. The Court may also issue detailed regulations as to the exchange of writings and even particularize the issues upon which the parties shall express themselves. However, a party may be directed to file more than one writing only for special cause.

### Section 11

If review dispensation is required, and the adverse party has been given an opportunity to respond, the Supreme Court shall determine, after the conclusion of the exchange of writings, whether such dispensation shall be granted. For cause, the matter of dispensation may be disposed of, although an exchange of writings has not occurred.

### Section 12

As to the proceedings in the Supreme Court in other respects, the provisions in chapter 52, sections 10–12, shall correspondingly apply.

### Section 13

After the Supreme Court has entered a final order, the files received from the court of appeals and copies of the order of the Supreme Court shall be returned, the court of appeals file to the appellate court and the lower court file to that court.

### Section 14

The provisions in this chapter shall correspondingly apply to limited appeals from decisions in accordance with chapter 8, section 8; in such appeals, however, the following diverging provisions shall govern:

1. A person desiring to appeal shall file a limited appeal petition with the Supreme Court within four weeks of service of the decision upon him.

2. Unless special reasons indicate otherwise, the complainant and, when the appeal is brought by the Attorney General, the adverse party as well shall be orally examined before the Supreme Court.

3. The organ of the Association of Advocates that rendered the decision appealed from shall be given an opportunity to file a written answer and, when a party is orally examined, to express its position on the matters raised in the examination. (SFS 1971:218)

# Chapter 57

## Actions Commenced in the Supreme Court

### Section 1

As to an action that is to be instituted in the Supreme Court as a court of first instance, the provisions in chapter 53 shall correspondingly apply.

# Part Seven

# Extraordinary Remedies

## Chapter 58

### Relief for Substantive Defects and Restoration of Expired Time

#### Section 1

After a judgment in a civil case has become conclusive, relief for a substantive defect in the judgment may be granted for the benefit of any of the parties:

1. if a member of the court or an official employed at the court rendered himself liable to criminal conduct or a misdemeanour in discharge of his duties with respect to the case, or if an attorney or legal representative was guilty of an offence with regard to the case, and the offence or misdemeanour can be assumed to have affected the outcome;

2. if a document presented as proof was forged or if a party examined under truth affirmation, or a witness, an expert or an interpreter gave false testimony, and the document or testimony can be assumed to have affected the outcome;

3. if a circumstance or evidence that was not presented previously is asserted, and presentation of the matter asserted would probably have led to a different outcome; or

4. if the application of law forming the basis of the judgment is obviously inconsistent with the governing legislative provision.

Relief for a substantive defect may not be granted on the basis stated in 3, unless the party makes it appear probable that he was unable to claim the circumstance or evidence in the court that pronounced the judgment or on appeal therefrom, or that on other grounds he had a valid excuse for failing to do so. (SFS 1975:670)

#### Section 2

After a judgment in a criminal case has become conclusive, relief for a substantive defect may be granted for the benefit of the defendant:

1. if a member of the court, an official employed at the court or the prosecutor rendered himself liable for criminal conduct or a misdemeanour in discharge of his duties with respect to the case, or if an attorney, legal representative or defence counsel was guilty of an offence with regard to the case, and the offence or misdemeanour can be assumed to have affected the outcome;

2. if a document presented as proof was forged or a witness, an expert or an interpreter gave false testimony, and the document or testimony can be assumed to have affected the outcome;

3. if a circumstance or evidence that was not presented previously is asserted, and presentation of the matter asserted would probably have led to the defendant's acquittal or to application of a sentencing provision milder than that applied; relief may also be granted if, in view of the new matter and other circumstances, extraordinary cause warrants a new trial on the question whether the defendant committed the crime for which he was convicted; or

4. if the application of law forming the basis of the judgment is obviously inconsistent with the governing legislative provision. (SFS 1975:670)

**Section 3**

After a judgment in a criminal case has become conclusive, relief for a substantive defect may be granted to the detriment of the defendant:

1. if a condition of the kind referred to in section 2, 1 or 2, existed, and the condition can be assumed to have contributed to the defendant's acquittal, or to application of a sentencing provision fundamentally milder than the one that should have been applied; or

2. if the offence is punishable by imprisonment for a term exceeding one year, and a circumstance or evidence that was not presented previously is asserted, and presentation of the matter asserted probably would have led to conviction of the defendant or to application of a sentencing provision fundamentally more severe than the one applied.

Relief for a substantive defect may not be granted on the basis stated in 2 unless the party makes it appear probable that he was unable to claim the circumstance or evidence in the court that pronounced the judgment or on appeal therefrom, or that on other grounds he had a valid excuse for failing to do so. (SFS 1964:166)

**Section 4**

A person desiring to apply for relief for a substantive defect shall file a written application therefor with the Supreme Court.

Applications in civil cases based upon a situation of the kind referred to in section 1, first paragraph, 1, 2, or 3, and applications in criminal cases to the detriment of the defendant, shall be submitted within one year of the time when the situation justifying the application became known to the applicant; if the application is based upon the criminal activity of another person, the period may be computed from the time when the judgmen in question became conclusive. In civil cases, relief based on a situation of the kind referred to in section 1, first paragraph shall be sought within six months of the time when the judgment became conclusive.

**Section 5**

In the application for relief for a substantive defect the applicant shall specify:

1. the challenged judgment;

2. the legal basis of, and supporting reasons for, the application; and

3. the evidence upon which the applicant desires to rely, and what he intends to prove by each specified item.

If the application is based upon matters stated in section 1, first paragraph 3, or section 3, first paragraph, 2, the applicant shall state why the circumstance or evidence was not presented in the proceedings.

The application shall be signed by the applicant or his attorney in his own hand.

The original or a certified copy of any document asserted by the applicant shall be annexed to the application.

**Section 6**

If an application for relief for a substantive defect is not dismissed, the application, with the papers annexed thereto, shall be served upon the adverse party with a notice directing him to file a written answer. If the application is found to be without merit, however, it may be dismissed forthwith.

The provisions in chapter 56, sections 9, 10, and 12 conserning limited appeals to the Supreme Court shall correspondingly apply to applications for relief for substantive defects.

For cause, the Supreme Court may direct that, until otherwise ordered, no further step may be taken to execute the judgment.

**Section 7**

If an application for relief for a substantive defect is granted, the Supreme Court shall direct that the case be taken up anew by the court in which it was last pending; however, when such relief is granted in a civil case, or in a criminal case for the benefit of the defendant, and the matter is found to be plain, the Supreme Court may change the judgment immediately.

If the applicant fails to appear at the hearing for readjudication of the action, the proceedings shall be dismissed; if the adverse party fails to appear, the action may nonetheless be retried and determined. The notices to appear served on the parties shall contain a reminder of the consequences of failure to appear. However, the provisions of this paragraph are not applicable to prosecutors.

**Section 8**

If an application for relief for a substantive defect is dismissed or denied, the Supreme Court may order the applicant to compensate the adverse party or, if the prosecutor is the adversary, the Treasury for costs incurred in the extraordinary remedy proceeding; if the relief was sought by the prosecutor, the costs may be paid out of public funds. If the application is granted, the issue of costs shall be determined in conjunction with the disposition of the case after its reinstatement.

**Section 9**

If a judgment in a criminal case also encompasses a matter other than criminal liability, relief for a substantive defect as to that part of the case shall be governed by the provisions for relief in civil cases; however, as an exception to this rule, if relief is granted on the question of criminal liability, relief may also be granted at the same time on any other aspect of the case.

**Section 10**

The provisions in sections 1–9 concerning judgments shall correspondingly apply to court orders.

**Section 11**

If the time has expired for an appeal from a judgment or an order, or for an application for reopening or reinstatement, and the person who failed to act within the period specified by statute was prevented from doing so by a circumstance that constitutes legal excuse, upon an application made by him the expired time may be restored, provided that the legal excuse was such that the person could not notify the court thereof prior to the expiration of the specified period.

### Section 12

A person who desires to apply for the restoration of expired time shall file a written application therefor with the Supreme Court within three weeks of the termination of the legal excuse and, at the latest, within one year of the expiration of the time period.

As to such applications, the provisions in section 5, 6, and 8 shall correspondingly apply.

## Chapter 59

### Relief for Grave Procedural Errors

### Section 1

A judgment that has become conclusive shall be vacated for grave procedural errors on the limited appeal petition of the person whose legal right the judgment concerns:

1. if the action was adjudicated on the merits, although a procedural hindrance existed that a higher court is obliged to notice on appeal on its own motion;

2. if the court was improperly constituted;

3. if the judgment was directed against someone who was not properly summoned and did not appear in the proceedings, or if the substantive rights of a person who was not a party to the action are adversely affected by the judgment;

4. if the judgment is so vague or incomplete that the determination on the merits cannot be ascertained therefrom; or

5. if another grave procedural error occurred in the course of the proceeding that can be assumed to have affected the outcome of the action.

### Section 2

A person desiring to take a limited appeal for relief from a grave procedural error shall file a limited appeal petition with the court to which an appeal from the judgment should have been brought or, if the judgment was not reviewable, with the Supreme Court.

If based on a circumstance of the kind referred to in section 1, 1, 2, or 5, the limited appeal shall be brought within six months after the judgment became conclusive and, if based on a circumstance of the kind referred to in section 1, 3, within six months of the time when the complainant learned of the judgment. If the complainant knew of the judgment before it became conclusive, the time shall be computed from the day when the judgment became conclusive.

**Section 3**

As to limited appeals for relief from grave procedural errors and further appeals from court of appeals orders on such matters, the provisions in chapters 52, 54 and 56 shall correspondingly apply; however, concerning limited appeals for such relief that are brought directly to the Supreme Court, the provisions for review dispensation shall not govern.

For cause, the court may direct that, until otherwise ordered, no further step be taken to execute the judgment in question.

If the judgment is vacated, except when the decision is grounded upon the court's lack of competence or upon another basis for concluding that the court should not have entertained the case on the merits, the vacation order shall direct that new proceedings occur in the court that rendered the judgment from which relief was granted.

As to compensation for expenses, the provisions for litigation costs shall apply. (SFS 1971:218)

**Section 4**

The provisions in sections 1–3 concerning judgments shall correspondingly apply to court orders.

**Section 5**

An order of summary punishment by fine consented to by the suspect shall be set aside upon a limited appeal:

1. if the consent cannot be considered a valid voluntary declaration of intent by the suspect;

2. if an error occurred during the processing of the matter of such character that the order should be considered invalid; or

3. if the order is otherwise inconsistent with the governing legislative provision.

If an order for summary punishment by fine is set aside, a more severe punishment for the same criminal act may not thereafter be imposed. (SFS 1959:257)

**Section 6**

A person who desires to attack an order of summary punishment by fine shall file a petition with the lower court that had competence to entertain a prosecution for the offence.

The petition shall be filed within one year after a step was taken against the suspect to execute the order. As to such petitions, the provisions in chapter 52, sections 2, 3 and 5–12 shall correspondingly apply. Any provision relating to a court of appeals, however, shall apply to the lower court. (SFS 1966:249)

**Section 7**

As to appeals from lower court determinations on petitions attacking orders for summary punishment by fine, the provisions in chapters 49 and 52 shall correspondingly apply.

Orders of the courts of appeals on such petition are not reviewable. (SFS 1966:249)

**Section 8**

In the situations referred to in sections 6 and 7, for cause, the court may direct that, until otherwise ordered, no further step may be taken to execute an order for summary punishment by fine. (SFS 1966:249)

**Section 9**

The provisions in sections 5–8 apply correspondingly in an issue concerning limited appeal from a summary imposition of a breach-of-regulations fine to which the suspect has given his consent. In a limited appeal from such summary imposition the public prosecutor is the suspect's adversary. (SFS 1968:193)

## Reports published in English by the NCCP

No 1 Non-Institutional Treatment – a preliminary evaluation of the Sundsvall experiment
No 2 General Deterrence
A conference on current research and standpoints June 2–4, 1975
No 3 Labeling Theory
– a critical examination
No 4 Deprivation of Freedom and the Police – an evaluation of the temporary custody act
No 5 A New Penal System
Ideas and Proposals
No 6 Police and the Social Order –
Contemporary Research Perspectives
No 7 Non-Institutional Treatment and Rehabilitation
An evaluation of a Swedish correctional experiment. Shortened version
No 8 Computer Technology and Computer Crime
No 9 Crime Prevention
No 10 Drug Criminality and Drug Abuse in Sweden 1969 – 1981
No 11 Current Swedish Legislation on Narcotics and Psychotropic Substances
No 12 Crime and Criminal Policy in Sweden
No 13 The Swedish Penal Code
No 14 Operation Identification – a way to prevent burglaries?
No 15 Everyday Violence in Contemporary Sweden. Situational and Ecological Aspects